## Discovering Shakespeare

# Much Ado About Nothing

## A WORKBOOK FOR STUDENTS AND TEACHERS

# Much Ado About Nothing

## A WORKBOOK FOR STUDENTS AND TEACHERS

Written and Edited by Rick Hamilton
and Fredi Olster

*Young Actors Series*

SK

A Smith and Kraus Book

A Smith and Kraus Book
Published by Smith and Kraus, Inc.
One Main Street, PO Box 127, Lyme, NH 03768

First Edition: August 1998
10 9 8 7 6 5 4 3 2 1

Library of Congress Cataloging-in-Publication Date

Hamilton, Rick.
Much ado about nothing: a workbook for students and teachers / by Rick Hamilton and Fredi Olster. —1st ed.
p. cm. —(Young actors series. Discovering Shakespeare series)
Includes bibliographical references.
Summary: Presents an abridged version of Shakespeare's Much ado about nothing,
discussing the play's language, characters, plot,
and how to stage a school production.
ISBN 1-57525-143-4

1. Shakespeare, William, 1564–1616. Much ado about nothing—
problems, exercises, etc.–Juvenile literature.
[1. Shakespeare, William, 1564–1616. Much ado about nothing.
2. Shakespeare, William, 1564–1616–Dramatic production.
3. Theater–Production and direction.
4. Plays–Production and direction.]
I. Hamilton, Rick.
II. Title
III. Series.

PR2828.H35    1998
822.3'3–dc21    98-7822
CIP
AC

# Contents

# "How came these things to pass?"

## HOW THESE BOOKS CAME TO BE WRITTEN

I have spent most of my life working as a Shakespearean actress. Yet, when I was growing up and studying Shakespeare in school, I hated it! I came to realize that many of my teachers also hated it. And who can blame any of us, we didn't understand it for the most part.

It wasn't until I started acting in Shakespeare's plays at the Oregon Shakespeare Festival in 1970 that I began to feel differently. There, I met Angus Bowmer, the founder of the festival and director of the first play I was to do there, *The Merchant of Venice*, and Rick Hamilton, a young actor at the festival, who was later to become my husband.

Between them, they taught me to love the language and to appreciate the timelessness of the stories. And now, of course, I'm hooked. I would rather act in a play by Shakespeare than any other playwright.

I've come to realize that my experience with Shakespeare is not unique. And it was my desire to share what I have learned from Angus and Rick and the many other directors and actors I've worked with over the years that inspired me to write this workbook.

The immediate impetus came, though, while I was doing a production of *Christmas Carol* in San Francisco. I was playing Mrs. Fezziwig, who is a delightful character but who isn't in a lot of scenes. So I had a great deal of time for other activities.

One of them was to start work on *All's Well That Ends Well*, which I was to be in when *Christmas Carol* closed. *All's Well* was a play that I was totally unfamiliar with. I was sitting in my dressing room with my Shakespeare glossaries, dictionaries, and various copies of the play doing my homework when my friend Sarah came in and asked what I was up to.

Sarah was then twelve and was playing Young Belle in our production. She and I were old friends, having worked together on two shows in the past. I told Sarah what I was doing, and she asked if she could read *All's Well* with me. I said "sure" and we proceeded to read the Helena/Parolles scene in Act 1 together.

Note that this is a particularly difficult scene, full of double-entendre, sexual innuendo, and very complex language. We read together and looked up all the words we didn't grasp.

Let me say here that I have to do this whenever I work on a Shakespeare play that I don't know well.

The words he used are different from the ones we now use. In the four hundred years since he wrote these plays, the English language has changed and some of the words Shakespeare used have gone out of fashion or have evolved in their meanings so that we no longer easily understand them.

But with a little practice and homework we quickly realize that the ideas he wrote about remain extremely applicable to us.

I came to understand this even more clearly when, after Sarah and I had finished the scene and had discussed what it meant, Sarah said to me, "I'm going to read this to my friends tomorrow at school, this stuff is great and it's so sexy." Well at that moment I realized once again the absolute brilliance of Shakespeare. He had the power to reach out through those four hundred years that separated him and Sarah and thoroughly excite her interest.

Sarah is now a young lady of fourteen and not only has she continued to be excited by Shakespeare, but she has passed on her interest to her younger sister Julia who is ten.

The question then became, how can we (by this time Rick agreed to work on this project with me) make Shakespeare accessible to kids who don't have an actor to sit down and read it with? And that's how the idea for this format came about.

Our objective became: tell the story, introduce the characters, and let Shakespeare's ideas come ringing through. The difficulty, of course, is that wonderfully complex language of Shakespeare's. So we decided the best way to introduce Shakespeare to people who were not familiar with him was, as I had done with Sarah, to translate him into the *vernacular*–that is, our equivalent everyday language.

That way, the new student of Shakespeare can begin to understand the story, the characters, and the ideas without the added obstacle of the four-hundred-year-old words.

Once these elements become clearer and the reader starts to discover the beauty of Shakespeare, as Sarah did, it then becomes even more thrilling to go back to the original language, which is, needless to say, so much richer and more poetic than anything we have replaced it with.

Let us point out here that this workbook is only meant as an introduction to Shakespeare. We are actors and not scholars and would not pretend competency in that world.

Our main objective is to instill a love of Shakespeare and to encourage the next generation of young people to attend our theaters with a true desire to see and support and perhaps act in the works of the incomparable master.

It is our sincere hope that the users of these workbooks will discover the joys of Shakespeare sooner than we were able to and will be tempted to move on to Shakespeare's complete versions of the plays with enthusiasm and ease.

# How to use this book

The Discovering Shakespeare edition of *Much Ado About Nothing,* with its abridged version of the play along with the vernacular translation and supportive chapters, is designed for multiple uses.

1. It serves as a workbook to help in the study of Shakespeare's language. By reading scenes aloud, and using the accompanying vernacular translation to facilitate comprehension, the student will find it easier to understand the language and plot of the play, thereby making the study of Shakespeare an enjoyable experience.
2. It serves as a launching pad for a *reading* of the play. Students take on the individual parts, doing research into the characters, and then, with scripts in hand, read the play aloud.
3. It serves as an aid in organizing a simple production of the play for classroom performance.

The facilities available and the needs and interests of the class will determine what would be most useful for the students.

We have included information about *performance* because we consider this material vital for the understanding of Shakespeare. Shakespeare was first and foremost a man of the theatre. To understand him, we feel it is necessary to have some understanding of the medium he was writing for.

It is our intention that the vernacular version will be employed to facilitate understanding of Shakespeare's language and that Shakespeare's own words be used for performance.

Also, please note that the suggested stage directions, acting notes, character interpretations, etc., reflect our personal opinions and should merely be thought of as a starting place. None of this is in stone; Shakespeare is open to interpretation. Be free and creative in your choices and your work.

You are the next generation of Shakespeare students, interpreters, audience, and performers. He is now in your hands—serve him well.

# "Was't not to this end that thou beganst to twist so fine a story?"

A DISCUSSION OF THE MAJOR THEMES OF *MUCH ADO ABOUT NOTHING*

BENEDICK:
Lady Beatrice, have you wept all this while?
BEATRICE:
Yea, and I will weep a while longer.
BENEDICK:
I will not desire that.
BEATRICE:
You have no reason, I do it freely.
BENEDICK:
Surely I do believe your fair cousin is wronged.
BEATRICE:
Ah, how much might the man deserve of me that would right her.
BENEDICK:
Is there any way to show such friendship?
BEATRICE:
A very even way, but no such friend.
BENEDICK:
I do love nothing in the world so well as you—is not that strange?
BEATRICE:
As strange as—the thing I know not. It were as possible for me to say I loved nothing so well as you—but believe me not—and yet I lie not—I confess nothing, nor I deny nothing. I am sorry for my cousin.
BENEDICK:
By my sword, Beatrice, thou lovest me.
BEATRICE:
Do not swear and eat it.
BENEDICK:
I will swear by it that you love me, and I will make him eat it that says I love not you.
BEATRICE:
Will you not eat your words?
BENEDICK:
With no sauce that can be devised. I protest I love thee.
BEATRICE:
Why then, God forgive me!
BENEDICK:
What offence, sweet Beatrice?

BEATRICE:

You have stayed me in a happy hour,
I was about to protest I loved you.

BENEDICK:

And do it with all thy heart.

BEATRICE:

I love you with so much of my heart that
none is left to protest.

BENEDICK:

Come, bid me do anything for thee.

BEATRICE:

Kill Claudio!

BENEDICK:

Ha! Not for the wide world!

BEATRICE:

You kill me to deny it. Farewell.

BENEDICK:

Tarry, sweet Beatrice.

BEATRICE:

I am gone, though I am here. There is
no love in you. Nay, I pray you let me go.

BENEDICK:

Beatrice—

BEATRICE:

In faith, I will go.

BENEDICK:

We'll be friends first.

BEATRICE:

You dare easier be friends with me than
fight with mine enemy.

BENEDICK:

Is Claudio thine enemy?

BEATRICE:

Is 'a not approved in the height a
villain, that hath slandered, scorned,
dishonored my kinswoman? O that I were
a man! What, bear her in hand until
they come to take hands, and then with
public accusation, uncovered slander,
unmitigated rancor—O God that I were
a man! I would eat his heart in the
marketplace.

BENEDICK:

Hear me, Beatrice—

BEATRICE:

Talk with a man out at a window! A proper
saying!

BENEDICK:

Nay, but Beatrice—

BEATRICE:

Sweet Hero! She is wronged, she is
slandered, she is undone.

BENEDICK:

Beat—

BEATRICE:

Princes and counties! A goodly count! O
that I were a man for his sake, or that
I had any friend would be a man for my
sake! But manhood is melted into curtsies,
valor into compliment, and men are turned
into tongue. He is now as valiant as
Hercules that tells a lie and swears it.
I cannot be a man with wishing, therefore
I will die a woman with grieving.

BENEDICK:

Tarry, good Beatrice, by this hand I
love thee.

BEATRICE:

Use it for my love some other way than
swearing by it.

BENEDICK:

Think you in your soul the Count Claudio
hath wronged Hero?

BEATRICE:

Yea, as sure as I have a thought or a
soul.

BENEDICK:

Enough! I am engaged, I will challenge
him. I will kiss your hand, and so I leave
you. By this hand, Claudio shall render
me a dear account. Go comfort your cousin.
I must say she is dead—and so farewell.

This sounds not like a comedy! Nevertheless it is. This is comedy by the mature Shakespeare. His concerns are becoming darker and more serious as he himself is growing older. He is no longer content to revisit Roman farces as he did in *Comedy of Errors,* or the commedia dell'arte in *The Taming of the Shrew.* He is now more interested in investigating that old show business saying, "comedy is serious business."

*Much Ado* is often called a romantic comedy—and in some aspects it is. "Boy meets girl, boy gets girl, boy loses girl, boy gets girl back." This is a formula common to many plays about love. One of the couples in *Much Ado* follows this course of events pretty closely. Shakespeare, though, takes this form and fills it with content that brings the boy and girl in question to the brink of tragedy. They are saved from serious consequences by some of the silliest nonsense you can imagine.

The other couple whose story we follow is more unconventional. Theirs is more of a "last chance at love" scenario following the "she hates him—he hates her—they must be in love" format. In both cases, however, hard lessons have to be learned, particularly by the men, to help them form a more perfect union!

But Shakespeare has too much to say to merely create a simple romantic comedy. As we shall see,

*Much Ado* is perhaps more of a satirical comedy of manners—satire being the use of wit, irony, or sarcasm to expose human folly.

The scene quoted above is a perfect example of this more serious style of comedy that Shakespeare is now writing. The scene can be played to huge laughs or to stunned silence; the debate about which way is best has been going on for four hundred years.

This scene is a masterful knitting together of two of the major themes of the play: honor and love. So how does this funny, high-spirited play come to such a seemingly serious pass? Let's briefly look at what the play is about in general terms, and then zero in on Shakespeare's main concerns.

The play's title immediately gives us some clues as to what's going on. "There's a double meaning in" it. To the Elizabethan, the words *nothing* and *noting* were pronounced very much the same. To *note* something is to pay it more than routine attention. You can note an idea, a pretty girl, or perhaps a conversation between others. Noting can be accidental or intentional. Its motive can be for good or evil purposes. But in any case, something has made you sit up and take notice!

*Much Ado* is full of examples of noting. It would seem that the people in Messina do little else but listen in on each other's conversations. Much of what is noted concerns other people's love affairs. Love has always made the world go round, and people have always been curious about it.

The more familiar pronunciation of the *nothing* in the title describes what most of the people in the play are actually taking note of—nothing! Nothing in the sense that almost everything that is overheard or noted is based on a deception of some sort and therefore has nothing to do with what really is!

Just about every character in the play is a victim of some sort of misperception, misnoting, or downright deception. Some of these are purely accidental, some are well-intentioned, and some are out-and-out malicious. For example: Antonio's being misled into believing that Don Pedro is in love with Hero because of a conversation misheard in his orchard is an innocent mistake. Benedick overhearing Claudio, Don Pedro, and Leonato talking about how much Beatrice loves him in his "gulling" scene is a well-meant ruse. Beatrice noting Hero and Ursula describing how lovesick Benedick is for her is the same. On the other hand, Claudio and Don Pedro being led to believe that Hero is talking to a man outside her chamber window, is an example of an evil-intentioned act. So what we have here is a whole lot of uproar based on some very flimsy reality or, as Shakespeare puts it, *Much Ado* about absolutely nothing.

*Much Ado* also deals with the way people use language. For some of the characters, language as a mere tool of communication is not enough. For them, using language brilliantly has become an end in itself. The ability to weave verbal tapestries of grace and charm is something to be cultivated. Content mattered, of course, but brilliant prattle was applauded and preferred to stumbling sincerity. Beatrice and Benedick are smashing, slashing, clashing examples of this. They are armored knights of wit and verbal prowess.

Dogberry is also a lover a language. He too loves to talk, and he uses language to display what he believes is his superior wit and intelligence and to try to elevate his place in society. Unfortunately in his case, he is seriously deluding himself. He and his cohorts in the Watch butcher the English language almost beyond recognition—they flat out draw and quarter it—so much so that not only we, but the characters who have to deal with him, are in need of a reference guide to decipher his meaning.

On the other hand, Shakespeare has given us characters who seem to disdain language. Don John's "I thank you, I am not of many words but I thank you," demonstrates language used for no other reason than to comply with necessity. Claudio goes one step further when he says, after a pause, "Silence is the perfectest herald of joy." (How unfortunate—a few words between Claudio and Hero before the wedding might have prevented much pain.)

Noting, nothing, and language are issues that serve to make the play amusing, witty, and even silly, but underlying all this joyous confusion are three areas of genuine concern to Shakespeare: honor, love, and reason. Let's explore each of these in turn.

## HONOR

Shakespeare had a bee in his bonnet about honor and the way in which people behaved because of it. Codes of honor have arisen in societies all over the world, but for our purposes, let's confine our investigation to Greece, Rome, and medieval Europe.

According to the Greek philosopher, Aristotle, honor was the logical result of living a virtuous life. A virtue is a specific moral quality regarded as good or meritorious. The virtues Aristotle had in mind were valor (courage in battle), honesty, loyalty, magnanimity (a kind of generosity of spirit), and an all-around good citizenship.

A man who was able to put all these virtues into practice and live by them would be regarded as an honorable man and be held in high esteem by his fellows. This became a prize, highly sought after and coveted. It is important to remember, however, that to

Aristotle living virtuously was what was important, not the honor that resulted from this way of life.

Also note that the root word of virtue is *vir,* meaning *man.* Virtue and honor, as described here, were a man's domain. Women's honor consisted only of chastity before marriage, faithfulness in marriage, and modesty at all times.

As Greece's power waned and Rome's came to fullness, this Aristotlean code of honor was transferred almost verbatim to the Roman culture. It remained an ideal for the Roman aristocracy for hundreds of years, though its emphasis on the approval of one's fellow-man brought it into conflict with the newly rising Christian church, which insisted that one should seek approval only from God.

As the Roman Empire came to an end, so too did its code of honor. It would lie dormant for almost a thousand years. But more on that later.

After the fall of Rome, conditions all over what we now call Europe changed. As the Germanic tribes, who had overrun the Roman lands, settled down on their newly won territory, they brought with them their own version of honor. They were a warrior society and theirs was an honor based on the glories of war and absolute loyalty to the man you served under.

The men who fulfilled the military needs of the society were given the most elevated status. They were awarded control of land and the people who lived on the land in exchange for supplying men and arms in times of war. These men became known as aristocrats, and they were the rulers of the society. Their view of the world was, "we fight and protect society, therefore we should be honored."

The two systems of honor mentioned above had similarities and also important differences. They both valued the accrual of honor and its attendant approval by one's fellow man. They differed, though, in that the Greco-Roman system had been carefully reasoned by the finest philosophers of its time to provide an ethical framework for virtuous behavior. If followed, this would lead to the accrual of honor. The medieval system, on the other hand, had no philosophical underpinnings but was merely the expression of a culture that valued military prowess and might.

Around the year 1400 (the beginning of the Renaissance), something happened that would unite these two systems of honor and breed a hybrid system that came to be known as the Renaissance Code of Honor. Aristotle was rediscovered, as were many other Greek and Roman writers. In fact, the entire pagan world began to reemerge. People all over Europe became fascinated by pre-Christian thinking. The Greco-Roman Code of Honor became the anthem of the European aristocracy.

Here was a Greek philosopher who, with unimpeachable reasoning, told them that everything they had thought about themselves all along was true. What could be better than that? Aristotle said valor is a virtue. Well, what else did aristocrats do but fight? Honest? Who dared say otherwise? Loyal? They had been swearing oaths of allegiance for hundreds of years. As for magnanimity, what nobleman wasn't magnanimous?

In the process of uniting the two honor systems, however, a huge mistake was made. Aristotle's emphasis on virtuous conduct as the vehicle by which one earned honor was distorted. What emerged in its place was the assumption that an aristocrat was born already possessing honor. This put a new slant on things. Men were now looking around to see if anyone was treating them with disrespect thereby affronting their innate, inborn honor, rather than being virtuous and earning their honor the old-fashioned way.

Rules and regulations about honor proliferated. They were to ensure that no disrespect was shown to any honorable man. Some fifty books were written during this time detailing the rules of honor that must be followed so as not to cause any insult or, if God forbid an insult is given, how to exact revenge. The slightest insult or sign of disrespect could cause you to lose honor and that could not be tolerated. Either the offender must apologize or he must be punished. This was done by challenging him to a duel. Not only did you avenge your honor this way, but if you won, you got more!

As you can imagine, things began to get a little out of hand. Shakespeare had had enough. He began to write plays that chronicled just how absurd the situation had become.

## LOVE

By the year 1100, the European aristocracy had gotten itself into a trap of its own making. The problem was with the way in which it dealt with love and marriage. Love was almost always ignored when making marriages. Instead, marriage was used to unite wealthy, politically powerful families. It is easy to see that marriage without love can lead to looking for love outside the marriage. This is where the problem lay. Adultery was a sin, a serious sin. To a society as religious as the one in the early Middle Ages, this presented a dilemma. Fortunately, change was beginning to occur. The aristocracy was beginning to be more and more independent of the church, and the church was beginning to be a little less rigid.

Into this situation came one of the most remarkable people of the Middle Ages. Her name was Eleanor. She was heiress to the richest piece of land in France—the Aquitaine. Born in 1122, she married King Louis VII of France at the age of fifteen, bore him two daughters, divorced him, and was married to Henry II, King of England, all by the time she was thirty. She bore him four sons, two of whom became kings of England themselves. By the time she was fifty, she had separated from her second husband and was living in the Aquitaine again, and changing the course of European history.

The Aquitaine (the southwest portion of France) has long been the home of radical ideas about religion and love. These ideas include an open acceptance of romantic love outside marriage. This is explosive stuff! Eleanor was able to transform what amounts to adultery in the eyes of the church into a code of love that embraces all the passion, all the yearning, all the exquisite misery of love without the sexual consummation—at least in theory!

During the years from 1168 to 1174, Eleanor ruled the Aquitaine in her own name. The principles of her rule were to be found in the wisdom of goddesses, not gods. She was able to gather most of the next generation of kings and queens of England, France, the Netherlands, and western Germany under her tutelage. What she taught them has become known as the Art of Courtly Love.

At the court of love, a man swore his oath of allegiance to his lady, he pledged to become her vassal (servant), she, his suzerain (master). The man humbled himself and begged to be accepted into her favor—not for her favors, but for her love. He wrote poetry to his lady. He offered to be her champion and asked her to set a deed or quest for him to complete. This trial that the man underwent would prove that his love was true. Love will complete them both. She will gain power. He will gain grace.

The following is a possible scenario of how love might come to flower in Eleanor's court.

A young knight, who has been sent to Eleanor's court to serve and learn attends his first grand ball. As he is standing with the other young knights, he catches sight of what he first thinks is an angel. The music fades, candle light dims, he finds himself hearing only his own heart beat as he seems to float across the room toward the vision he has seen. As he draws near, his heart rate increases, and the angel turns and looks straight into his eyes. Night becomes day, his heart is as big as the room—he finds himself standing too close to be ignored. Suddenly Queen Eleanor turns, looks at him, smiles, and with a sparkle in her eye says, "Ah, Count Jean, I would like you to meet the Duke and Duchess of Flanders." Polite greetings are made. Proper form is followed, but the bottom has fallen out. She's married; she will never be his. His joy evaporates, replaced by chilled empty space. He watches as the Duke and Duchess sweep off. The

angel, whose name is Rosamund, has given him not a flicker of hope, but her impact is permanent. Suddenly Queen Eleanor is speaking again, "Jean, you are pale. Have some cognac and then to bed and sleep, if you can." He can't.

The next morning, still awake, he is listening to the snores of the young knights he shares his room with. Hearing foot steps approaching, he goes to the door, and there is the captain of the Queen's guard who says, "Gather your belongings and follow me." Quietly, he does so. They go to another part of the castle, and the captain shows him a room that is to be his alone. Inside on the table is a letter and a small box. He opens the letter and reads,

*My dear Jean,*
*It is time you were alone with your heart. There is writing material on the table. When you have learned to put your heart on paper, your true heart, deliver the paper heart to whom it is intended. In the box, you will find a small knife and what is called a fork. They are for eating with. Learn to use them as skillfully as you use your sword and you will be amazed.*
*E.*

A week goes by with no sight of the angel. Only scribbling and practicing with his new found utensils. Another week. An invitation arrives asking him to a dinner. When he arrives, he realizes that he is one of the most insignificant people there. The angel is there, but she is so far away he can hardly see her. He has brought his own fork only to discover that the entire table is laid with them. Across the table and next to him are young men and women with wicked tongues and merry eyes. Jean is polite but focuses on his fork, trying not to drop anything. As the evening nears its end, an announcement is made. The Duke of Flanders is leaving to attend to some business on his lands and will be gone for some time. The Duchess will be staying, anxiously awaiting his return.

The next morning, as everyone else is bidding good-bye to the Duke, Jean enters his beloved's room. If he is caught, he is dead, but his love is stronger than his fear. He hides what he hopes is his "heart on paper" under her pillow and leaves.

Another week goes by, another invitation arrives. He is to attend that evening's "Court of Love." The Queen and her daughters have been considering a point of love that has been raised, and a verdict is about to be handed down. Dressed in his finest, Jean attends. An announcement is made that the judgment will be given at the end of the evening and until then the lords and ladies should enjoy themselves.

The evening commences with a meal. This time

Jean is seated closer to Rosamund. He is not close enough for conversation, but he can hear her laugh. By now he is an expert with knife and fork. He is speaking with the lady seated next to him when he notices Rosamund looking at him. He immediately stops talking and finishes his meal in silence.

The dinner ends and the court convenes. The evening's issue is a continuing discussion of character traits or dispositions that tend to act as a bar to love. Queen Eleanor rises from her throne and steps down to the audience. She says, "We have been discussing various impediments to love. This night I would like to speak briefly about a bar to love which seems to be prevalent among the young—excess of passion. An excess of passion is a bar to love because there are men who are slaves to such passionate desire that they cannot be held in the bonds of love. Men who, after they have thought long about some woman or even enjoyed her, upon seeing another woman, straightway desire her embraces. Men of this kind lust after every woman they see; their love is like that of a shameless dog. They should rather, I believe, be compared to asses, for they are moved only by that low nature which shows that men are on the level of the other animals rather than by that true nature which sets us apart from all the other animals by the difference of reason." *

Queen Eleanor thanks those in attendance for their attention and prays that they consider what has been spoken. She adds, "If there is another opinion, let it be stated tomorrow night." All bow to her as she leaves for her apartments. Jean, who has decided he can no longer stand not speaking to his love, searches for Rosamund but in vain; she is not to be found. He leaves the hall determined to find a way to deposit another poem in his lady's chamber.

As he exits the hall, he sees Rosamund coming toward him. She has no chaperone. She says, "Good even, Jean." Jean, bowing, his heart pounding, replies, "Good even, Milady. I'm glad to have found you. I wanted to speak to you." Rosamund says, "I'm glad you did find me, there is something I wished to tell you. As I was escorting Queen Eleanor to her rooms, she said that the skill you display with knife and fork is equal to the way in which you handle your sword." Jean, dumbfounded, stammers, "The Queen said that? When did she see me with my sword?" "We watched you practicing, 'twas two days ago. She said, too, that you sit well upon your horse." Jean, summoning his courage says, "How do you think I sit?" Rosamund, with a faint smile replies, "I think the Queen knows whereof she speaks." Jean, hardly believing what he is hearing, blurts out, "Had I known such an illustrious

*(From *The Art of Courtly Love* by Andreas Capellanus).

and lovely audience was present, I am certain I could have fought better." "I've no doubt. Good night, Jean, I must retire." Jean, not wanting the moment to end says, "Milady, may I escort you to your chamber?" Rosamund smiles, "There is no need, but I thank you." She leaves without offering her hand. Jean is in heaven and hell at the same time. He has spoken to her again. She has noticed him and approves but has withheld her hand. What does that bode? As he enters his room, his questions are answered. A note on his table reads, "Tomorrow at nine, ride north. R."

That night is spent cleaning everything: his horse, his saddle, his sword, his clothes, his hands—everything.

Next morning, after leaving the castle grounds and heading north, he spies a scarf loosely tied to a branch. It marks a trail into the forest, which he begins to follow. His mind and heart are racing, "What will happen? Will she be there?" As the trail curves, there is a sunlit opening in the forest canopy, and she is there, upon her horse, waiting, alone. How could she risk this? The tightness in his chest lets go, and tears begin cascading down his face. Through his tears he can see she is trembling. He leaps off his horse and kneels at her feet, and in spite of his tears and shortness of breath says, "You are my Goddess. I beg your forgiveness. I repent for my rashness, my daring to love such a one as you. My love cannot be reined in. I swear by the fire of love that burns in my heart that every act of my life, whether near or far, shall go to serving you. If I die for loving you, I am happy." Jean stops, he cannot go on. After a moment he looks up and sees that she too is in tears. She is luminous. He starts to rise, but in a strong clear voice she says, "No! Kneel, Jean." He does. "Do not look at me, just listen. I love you no less. Indeed there is no measure of my love, no measurer, not even God. But hear me. If our love is to mean anything, it must go no further. I will come to you in your dreams. I will leave you not even in death. But this must be our first and last kiss. Keep my scarf and wear it always, and know that I am with you. Now arise, my love, and brand my soul with your lips."

At this point we must leave our lovers to work out their own fate.

So what's going on here? Much ado about a lot. Eleanor is raising the status of women and refining the uncouthness of her time—all in the name of love! She attempted to establish a system whereby men and women could share love in its purest, most uplifting forms. If she was not entirely successful, there's no shame in that; nobody else has been either. Nobody! But we must admire her attempt.

Eleanor was able to maintain her court for only six years. In 1174 her husband, Henry II, had her confined to a castle. She remained there for over a decade. But she had planted her seeds, and they spread all over Europe. Her teachings would be interpreted on many levels. Some would find a religious aspect to love, some a refined sense of culture and manners, others would experience the elevated sense of passion that was possible between men and women. But for the first time in centuries, homage would be paid to the glory of women.

Over the next hundred and fifty years, the principles of feudal honor and courtly love would serve as the mainsprings of what was to be known as the Age of Chivalry. Not only would male/female relationships be affected, but European literature from the legends of King Arthur down to modern romances would be influenced by these ideas.

In their purest form, these ideals captured the hearts, minds, and imaginations of the people who came under their influence. The Greek, who was able to live according to the code of honor, was an example of the highest aspirations of his society. Life might be capricious, but he could remain true to his beliefs. The same could be said of the medieval knight who believed in the power of love. If he was able to radiate to the world around him the love that had been ignited by his beloved, his life might be a tiny spark of the divine fire. These were certainly worthy goals.

But just as we saw earlier with the ideals of the honor code, the principles of courtly love were to become distorted and perverted over time.

Aristocratic women, who had always been regarded as property by their husbands, were now being placed on pedestals and worshipped by their lovers. Neither point of view is a realistic assessment of what they are—human beings!

Another consequence of courtly love (and this was where the sublime became the ridiculous) was the dilemma of a noble lord who, after his consiousness had been raised by the purity of his passion for his beloved, was outraged to discover that his own wife had become the beloved of some other lord. Out of this grew the great fear of "cuckoldry," that dreaded condition of being the husband of an adulterous wife.

Courtly love was an ideal which was perhaps a little too lofty to be maintained by plain old human beings, and by Shakespeare's time it had become terribly debased. In *Much Ado* Shakespeare satirizes honor and courtly love, and with the creation of Beatrice and Benedick, he calls for the adoption of another Greek ideal to guide relationships between men and women—reason!

Shakespeare uses the character of Benedick to illustrate his thoughts about courtly love. Benedick starts out seeming to be anything but a lover. He tells us he is a "professed tyrant" to the female sex. He reasons that since women are not to be trusted, a man

could be made a cuckold by marrying, and he refuses to take that risk. But as soon as he falls in love, he completely reverses himself. He undergoes a transformation. As Claudio and Don Pedro note, he appears sad, (he's sighing); he becomes overly attentive to his clothing ("'A brushes his hat o' mornings"); he wears perfume; he's melancholy; and he's washing his face an awful lot. We even discover that he's been writing love poetry! These are all symptoms of being a courtly lover.

In the wedding scene, Benedick swears an oath of love to Beatrice, offers to become her champion, and asks her to bid him do anything for her. Honor and love become inextricably intertwined here. Once Beatrice and Benedick openly declare their love, they both fall victim to the precepts of the honor code. Benedick swears a solemn oath to his love and declares his willingness to "do anything" for his lady and Beatrice takes him up on his offer with the demand of "Kill Claudio!"

They have become "courtier" and "courted" in the very traditional sense of these words. Benedick suddenly finds himself enmeshed in Beatrice's desire to have Hero's honor avenged.

His struggle, "Hear me, Beatrice—," "Nay, but Beatrice—," "Beat—," to inject reason into the mix, is overcome by Beatrice's passionate call for revenge. He is now committed to her and there is no turning back. This is the culmination of Shakespeare's argument. All the elements: honor, love, and reason are now tightly compressed. They have reached critical mass and something's got to give! Reason is overwhelmed by passion; courtly love is subverted by honor; and honor is being used as a tool to exact revenge.

Through Beatrice's enraged attack on Claudio's behavior and on the completely degraded state of Elizabethan manhood ("Princes and counties! A goodly count! O that I were a man for his sake, or that I had any friend would be a man for my sake! But manhood is melted into curtsies, valor into compliment, and men are turned into tongue. He is now as valiant as Hercules that tells a lie and swears it"), Shakespeare is expressing his own disgust at the degradations of these ideals.

Don Pedro and Leonato must be included in Beatrice's diatribe. They have accepted the word of a proven villain, Don John, whose honor has already been repudiated. They are willing to do so because of their inherent distrust of women and their paranoia concerning the possible loss of their honor. Benedick is about to use honor to right the wrongs committed by Don Pedro and Claudio in the name of honor! This is fighting fire with fire.

Shakespeare clearly believes that something must be done. The heart of the matter is that the honor code has become so subverted that it no longer serves or can be admired in its present form. It is a system that needs to be reexamined. As it stands, it is a code that can destroy a young lady's life and can sever friendships with no real basis. It needs to be looked at and rethought—with reason!

Thank heaven for the Dogberry subplot, which inadvertently clears things up, or we'd have a tragedy on our hands. It is Shakespeare's genius of interweaving these plots that allows all to turn out well in this very dangerous situation. In his earlier play, *Romeo and Juliet*, both Tybalt and Mercutio are killed as a result of honor gone amok. But in *Much Ado*, comedy prevails and saves the day.

## REASON

In Act 5 scene 2, Beatrice and Benedick begin to create a new model of courtship for themselves. This one will be free of the old conventions. Benedick returns from his challenge of Claudio. He has completed his lover's task. As he is waiting for Beatrice, he tries to compose a love sonnet (a very courtly thing to do). But, try as he might, he must admit his failure. He cannot "show it in rhyme." With a sigh of relief, he gives up and puts the conventions of courtly love behind him. We will learn later that Beatrice too had tried and failed at the same convention. Theirs will have to be a courtship of another kind. They will continue their merry war of words, but with a difference—there is no longer any attempt to wound, but only to play.

In the final scene, they both state the terms of their new-found way of love. They will love—"no more than reason!" They will perhaps die for love, but only if sanity and reason have been consulted first!

# "Wooing, wedding, and repenting"
## ELIZABETHAN MARRIAGE CUSTOMS

In Elizabethan times, marriage among the upper classes was very different from what we are used to today. It's important to understand the expectations and limitations of these relationships in order to understand the world of *Much Ado*.

Marriages for upper class young men and women were usually arranged for them by their parents. Oftentimes these pairings were based solely on the desirability of joining aristocratic families for the purpose of reinforcing alliances between them, or to unite their land holdings. Love either came later, or did not come at all, depending on the couple.

The young woman was particularly vulnerable since she was totally ruled by her father and could be bartered as he saw fit. The obedient young woman of the day had little if any say as to whom she would marry. Beatrice refers to this when she says, "It is my cousin's duty to make curtsy and say, 'Father, as it please you.'" Hero, a proper young lady of the time, must go along with her father's choice.

The young man had more to gain in marriage since a dowry (monetary settlement) always went along with the young lady. This is why Claudio is so interested in whether Hero has any brothers. If she did, her dowry would probably be smaller.

In *Much Ado*, Don Pedro and Leonato reach an agreement regarding the marriage of Claudio of Hero. By the time Don Pedro tells Claudio, "I have wooed in thy name, and fair Hero is won. I have broke with her father and his good will obtained," contractual terms would have been agreed upon, including a financial settlement.

The *espousal* or public commitment made between Claudio and Hero in Act 2 scene 1, is considered binding under law. Claudio and Hero are, in effect, husband and wife. All that remains to be done is the actual ceremony.

Part of the contractual agreement would be that Hero is a virgin. When Claudio comes to believe, through Don John's deception, that this is not the case, his contract with Leonato would become nullified, and he would be justified in calling off the marriage.

The reason Hero's virginity is such an issue is not only that it was, first and foremost, the most precious possession a young lady could have at this time, but also that Leonato would have attested to it in the contract. If Hero were truly not virginal, Leonato's honor would be shamed. Don Pedro, who earlier told Claudio, "that she is worthy, I know," and then went on to "link [his] friend to a common stale" would be dishonored. Claudio himself, of course, would be dishonored in marrying damaged goods, and therefore is totally justified in rejecting "this rotten orange."

Hero's honor (reputation) has been destroyed in the eyes of the public. No respectable man would want to marry her now. This is why Beatrice is so vehement about wanting revenge.

This is a radically different attitude than exists today, and if we are not aware of the issues at stake in Elizabethan times, we cannot understand the reactions of the characters to what occurs in the play.

# "John the bastard, whose spirits toil in frame of villainies"

BASTARDY IN SHAKESPEARE'S DAY

There is a mistaken notion that being born a bastard in Shakespeare's time was a horrible blot that was impossible to overcome. This is not necessarily the case.

During the Elizabethan era, marriages were arranged for social and economic reasons rather than for the sake of love. So oftentimes a true love relationship was found outside the bonds of matrimony. The love children who were the result of these extra-marital affairs were frequently the favorites of their fathers because they were the product of that love affair between the man and his mistress.

As it became public knowledge that kings, dukes, and even popes were fathering illegitimate offspring, these bastards became more and more accepted. It was not unusual for these children to be elevated to high positions in society or in the church and to be given special mentions in their father's wills.

Philip, the Duke of Burgundy, a powerful and highly respected member of the French nobility, had seventeen bastard offspring. They were brought up alongside their legitimate brother, and all did very well in later life, achieving positions of respect. William the Conqueror was another famous bastard, as was the Bastard of Orleans who fought alongside Joan of Arc. Pope Innocent VIII was known to have had seven bastard offspring. King John (Eleanor of Aquitaine's son) even went so far as to give his many illegitimate children the last name of Fitzroy: *fils* means *sons* in French, and *roi* means *king*. Fitzroy therefore meant, sons of the King.

Bastards had a certain advantage in that they were in the unique position of being virtually independent. There were no legal bonds tying them to family. This meant not only that the child had no claim on the family wealth, but that the family had no claims on any wealth that the child might accrue. These free spirits were often looked upon as being rather glamorous and intriguing people.

So while Shakespeare paints Don John with the negative aspects one might associate with bastardy (mean-spiritedness, a sullen and sour disposition, a man out to get revenge on everyone), we see that he is not necessarily representative of illegitimate offspring of the time. Perhaps he's just a bastard!

# "The world must be peopled"

BRIEF DESCRIPTIONS OF THE CHARACTERS IN *MUCH ADO ABOUT NOTHING*

The Messina of *Much Ado* appears to be a rather charming town. It is friendly and peaceful. The Governor's household is a fairly informal place with servants and masters on familiar terms. The fact that Dogberry and Verges represent the law enforcement branch of Messina seems to indicate that crime is not a major social issue.

The social structure of the town emanates from Don Pedro, Prince of Aragon, under whose rule Messina sits. Everyone else in *Much Ado* owes allegiance to him. Benedick and Claudio are members of the upper class society. This, along with being Don Pedro's closest personal allies, sets them fairly high on the social ladder.

Locally, Leonato is the most prominent citizen since he is the Governor of Messina. His position reflects favorably on his family, giving them an elevated status in the community.

While Don John is brother to the Prince, his recent rebellion against him, along with his bastardy, leave him skirting the fringes of society.

Dogberry, Verges, the Watch, and the servants of Leonato's household all occupy lower class positions in society. And much as they strive to emulate the upper class, it is unlikely that they will ever achieve higher status than they were born into.

Conrade and Borachio, who were probably born into the merchant class, are definitely out of favor because of their associations with the shady Don John.

Members of the clergy might be thought to be above these societal machinations, but often the secular and religious realms overlapped. In the case of Friar Francis, he tries to maintain his clerical objectivity while making sure he does nothing to offend the Prince.

Let's take a look at all these characters individually and see what makes them tick and how they participate in the action of *Much Ado*.

[Note that it's best to read about all the characters, not just the one you might be playing. Not only are there clues about your character in another character's description, but the more you know about the other people in the play, the better you understand how to interact with them.]

## DON PEDRO

Don Pedro is the Prince of Aragon. Aragon rules Sicily at this time in history, thereby making Don Pedro the leader of this region. Everyone in this play owes their allegiance to him.

We quickly learn that Don Pedro has just squelched a rebellion led by his bastard brother, Don John. The fact that Don John is still around after stirring up this rebellion says a lot about Don Pedro's character. He has chosen not to execute his brother as he might have done, and though Don John seems to be under a sort of house arrest, he still has relative freedom.

Don Pedro is a powerful ruler who commands the respect of his subjects, as indicated by Leonato's deferential treatment of him, but he also allows for a great deal of informality. This respectful ease, obvious throughout the play, seems to indicate that Don Pedro is a successful yet benevolent ruler.

We note too that Don Pedro is most anxious to reward young Claudio for his heroic actions in the wars. He makes a point in his letter to Leonato of mentioning the honors already heaped on Claudio, and when Claudio asks Don Pedro for help in getting Hero's hand, Don Pedro is quick to assure Claudio that he is ready to do whatever he can for him. This is a sign of an honorable ruler. The Renaissance code of honor, to which Don Pedro faithfully adheres, not only required that the subject perform honorable service for his liege lord, but that the lord be ready and willing to reward such service.

Don Pedro is very attentive to details. Very little escapes his notice. His concern extends even to the love affairs of his subjects. As soon as he learns of Claudio's infatuation with Hero, he offers to help win her hand. He goes so far as to disguise himself and play Claudio's part in wooing Hero. He likes to get right in the thick of things.

He next turns his attention to Beatrice and Benedick. He can see that Beatrice is carrying a torch for Benedick. He also notes that Benedick is far too easily upset by Beatrice not to be in love with her. He decides to play Cupid and bring these two prickly pears together to grow side by side.

Don Pedro has several reasons for being so involved in his subjects' lives. He is very fond of them, and since he is in a position to do good for them, why not? Don Pedro loves to orchestrate the world around him, and he's good at it—it is the mark of a good ruler to be able to manipulate events. Also, Don Pedro is not married. Being a prince, he should at least make a political marriage, but he doesn't seem to have any prospects. There is a bit of a mystery here about Don Pedro. Perhaps he feels unworthy of love. Perhaps by bringing his favorite subjects together, he gets vicarious pleasure. Whatever the reason, Shakespeare gives us no clues. Don Pedro has a good heart and Messina is lucky to have him.

Why does Don Pedro choose to become so involved in his subjects' personal lives? To begin with, he is very fond of them and since he is in a position to do good for them, why not? Secondly, Don Pedro loves to orchestrate the world around him—he's good at it, and it is the mark of a good ruler to be able to manipulate events. And lastly, Don Pedro is a bachelor. Why this is, Shakespeare never tells us, but perhaps he fills some of his own needs for love by playing Cupid and helping sparks of love to fly between his favorite subjects. Whatever the reasons, Don Pedro has a good heart and Messina is lucky to have him.

But Don Pedro has a weakness, and it is revealed in the wedding scene. His Achilles' heel is his obsession with honor. The scheme concocted by Borachio and Don John to cast aspersions on Hero's reputation makes Don Pedro feel that his honor is stained because of his part in linking "his dear friend to a common stale." Since keeping his own honor pure is the most important thing to Don Pedro, he is easily drawn into Don John's trap.

It is Don Pedro's desire to protect his honor that explains his seemingly reprehensible behavior at the wedding and later with Leonato. It is not until he hears the news that his brother has fled that he begins to suspect the truth. When it is confirmed by Borachio's admission, this honorable Prince—who need not by law do anything—agrees to "bend under any heavy weight" to make amends to Leonato.

## DON JOHN

Don John is the bastard brother of Don Pedro, Prince of Aragon. They probably shared the same royal father, but different mothers.

The consequence of illegitimacy was that the bastard child could not legitimately lay claim to the lineage into which he was born. A bastard, therefore, could not have the full identity or acceptance in society that is granted to rightful heirs. A bastard son would forever be somewhat of an outcast in the eyes of society. Although they could, and often did, rise to positions of power, this was most often only achieved through the good graces of the legitimate family members.

When Leonato addresses Don John in the first scene of the play, he calls him "my lord." Leonato tells him that since he has become reconciled with his brother, the Prince, Leonato owes him duty. This indicates that Don John holds a position of respect, but only through Don Pedro's indulgence.

Don John has raised a rebellion against his brother, which Don Pedro and his troops have put down. Obviously the skirmish was sufficient enough to earn Claudio recognition for his courage, but the battle must not have been terribly long or bloody since it is noted that few lives were lost.

Don John is now smarting from his defeat. Not only has he lost in his attempt to overthrow his brother, but during the course of the action, he has watched as young Claudio garnered praise. As Don John says, "that young startup hath all the glory of my overthrow."

He may have been beaten in the war but not humbled. Don John is now like a coiled snake, waiting for the moment to strike. Even in the face of defeat, he is determined to stir up more trouble. He despises Claudio and would love to make his life miserable.

Don John has a decidedly sour disposition. Beatrice says, "How tartly that gentleman looks! I never can see him but I am heartburned an hour after." Don John is aware of his negative aura and perhaps even proud of it. He acknowledges that he is "a plain-dealing villain" and neither tries, nor desires, to hide that fact. He does not attempt to win honor through virtuous means, but rather tries to destroy those who have it. He is a melancholy, petty, destructive man.

His first attempt to cross things up comes when he finds Claudio alone after the dance. He tries to drive a wedge between Claudio and the Prince by insinuating that Don Pedro is actually in love with Hero and is courting her for himself. While the young and gullible Claudio takes up this bait, it ultimately does nothing for Don John because Don Pedro is able to show Claudio that, indeed, he has won Hero for his sake and gives her over to him. It is this sort of pettiness that Don John thrives at, but it takes the cleverness of his henchman Borachio to come up with something really daring.

Borachio suggests the plan to discredit Hero. Borachio knows that Don Pedro will feel as though his honor has been besmirched by attempting to marry his friend off "to a contaminated stale." But Borachio has to practically spell out the expected consequences of his plan before the malicious, but somewhat dim-witted, Don John catches on and decides to go along.

In Act 3 scene 2, Don John sets the plan in motion with a convincing show of concern for Claudio's reputation and, with terse but plausible statements, plays his part at the wedding.

Though he does not appear again after the wedding scene, his spiteful aura hangs over much of the ensuing action until it is finally reported that this treacherous little man has snuck off from Messina.

## CLAUDIO

Claudio is one of those young men who seems to have everything going for him. He's young, he's handsome and he's just made a big heroic splash in the wars.

Before he ever appears in the play, we learn that Don Pedro has "heaped high praise" on Claudio for his triumphs in the wars, "doing in the figure of a lamb, the feats of a lion."

The Renaissance code of honor to which Claudio adheres required that a young man accrue as much honor for himself as he could. Claudio is a very typical young man of his time. He is interested in getting ahead, and he does this by performing admirably in the wars, thus receiving the recognition of his liege lord, Don Pedro. Having accomplished this, he feels it's time to make an honorable marriage, thereby reinforcing his fortune and establishing his place in society.

Claudio doesn't utter a word in the play until he is alone with Benedick. He then brings up Hero, who Claudio believes "is the sweetest lady that [he] ever looked on." We should take particular note of the phrase "looked on," because Claudio and Hero have not said a word to each other. We later discover that Claudio had "looked upon her with a soldier's eye" before going off to war, but again he says nothing about having ever talked to the lady! We will come to realize that Claudio is more in love with his image of Hero, than with the lady herself.

Claudio knows that Hero comes from a good family, but he obviously doesn't know much else about her. He has to ask Don Pedro if she has any brothers. This is a very important question for a young gentleman who is looking to get ahead. If Hero did have brothers, they would inherit most of the family fortune.

Once it is established that Hero is Leonato's only heir, Claudio is intent on making her his wife. A good marriage to an honorable young lady will not only cement his social standing, but increase his fortunes. Don Pedro senses Claudio's desire for assistance and offers to "break with her and with her father" for him. Claudio is delighted and off they go.

But Claudio is young and gullible, and when the malicious Don John tries to stir up trouble by insinuating that Don Pedro is courting Hero for himself, Claudio falls for it and slumps off to lick his wounds. It is important to note these aspects of Claudio's character. These are the same character traits that will later allow him to fall victim to Don John's lies about Hero.

When Don Pedro convinces Claudio that he has acted on his behalf, we witness Claudio's tongue-tied silence as he stands face-to-face with the lady he is about to marry, but barely knows.

Claudio is perfectly comfortable in the Benedick gulling scene, joking and having a good time with the guys. This is the Claudio who Benedick got to be pals with during the wars. We realize that Claudio is one of those young men who is perfectly relaxed with other men, but hasn't a clue what to say to a lady.

In Act 3 scene 2, it's interesting to note that

Claudio is willing to abandon his bride after the ceremony. He offers to accompany Don Pedro to Aragon. We again realize that it is the idea of love and marriage with Hero that Claudio is attracted to, and not Hero herself. So when Don John tells him that "the lady is disloyal," we can more easily understand Claudio's dilemma. He doesn't know anything about Hero except what he has been told by others. Why shouldn't he believe this too—especially after his eyes are deceived by the charade that Borachio and Margaret create at Hero's bedroom window?

Much as we would like Claudio to protest Hero's innocence, all he can see is that his honor was nearly destroyed by marrying her. He thought he was getting choice goods and all she turned out to be was a "rotten orange"! He feels angry and deceived and he wants it publicly acknowledged that he is totally in the right and she, totally wrong.

When he is later confronted by Leonato, his self-righteous superiority allows him to rebuff the "old man." It is only when Benedick appears and Claudio tells him that he is "high-proof melancholy" that we realize that the events at the wedding have had some impact on him. But when Benedick calls Claudio a villain and challenges him to a duel to avenge Hero's honor, Claudio cannot believe his ears. Claudio sincerely believes that he is the injured party in all this.

It is not until Borachio reveals the true circumstances of the events witnessed at Hero's window that Claudio realizes the depth of his mistaking. But note that even here he says, "Sweet Hero, now thy image doth appear in the rare semblance that I loved at first." He is still obsessed with the *image* of Hero.

When Claudio submits himself to whatever revenge Leonato chooses, Leonato wisely decides to test Claudio. He requires him to publicly admit his part in Hero's death by telling the "people in Messina how innocent she died," and then by having Claudio promise to marry, sight unseen, Antonio's daughter.

By agreeing to these terms, Claudio demonstrates his willingness to take responsibility for his actions—a big step toward his maturity. So that when Claudio discovers that his bride is actually the Hero who he believed he'd lost, we can feel that there is hope for this marriage.

## LEONATO

Leonato is the governor of Messina. He seems to be a good-natured gentleman, content in his life and his family. When we meet him in the first scene, he has just received the news that Don Pedro will shortly be arriving in Messina. When he appears, Leonato is extremely gracious in receiving him.

We also witness Leonato's easy good-humor.

When Don Pedro says, "I think this is your daughter," Leonato responds with, "Her mother hath many times told me so"—an old joke, but evidence of Leonato's light-hearted spirit. And when Benedick comes back with the jibe, "Were you in doubt, sir, that you asked her?" Leonato answers him with, "no—for then were you a child." Leonato enjoys this easy banter and is looking forward to having the opportunity to entertain his guests as lavishly as he can.

Our next encounter with him is when Antonio comes to report what was overheard by his servant. The servant told Antonio (incorrectly of course) that the Prince was in love with Hero and was going to propose that very night. Leonato, excited by the prospect of being related to the royal family, decides to tell Hero of this news so she will be prepared to answer yes if this comes to pass.

This misunderstanding about who is actually going to propose to his daughter is cleared up offstage and Leonato accepts the idea of a count as his son-in-law with equal joy. His only concern is that he be given adequate time for the wedding preparations.

The business now turns to the Prince's suggestion of getting Benedick and Beatrice together. Leonato seems very happy at this prospect. We've seen glimpses of Leonato's relationship with Beatrice: when he explains Beatrice's strange behavior to the Messenger in the first scene, when he gently scolds Beatrice for her shrewd tongue, and when he intercedes in the quasi-proposal moment between Beatrice and Don Pedro and finds an excuse to send Beatrice out of the room. Leonato appears to personally enjoy his niece's wit and charm, but seems somewhat uncomfortable knowing that she can go too far at times.

The prospect of marrying Hero and Beatrice off must be a happy one for Leonato—it would be the fulfillment of a father's/guardian's responsibility to know that his young ladies will be taken care of when he is gone.

It's a delight to watch Leonato take part in Benedick's gulling scene. We watch as he valiantly tries to play the part that Don Pedro has devised for him in this little skit. The fact that Benedick says, "I should think this a gull, but that the white-bearded fellow speaks it," makes us realize that even though Leonato may not be the best at play-acting, he is surely respected for his sincerity and honesty.

It is at the wedding that we see a darker side of Leonato. When Hero's honor is brought into question by Claudio and the Prince, Leonato responds in a way that is shocking to modern audiences. Elizabethans though, understood his reaction, realizing that if Hero was guilty as accused, she had not only ruined her own reputation, but had stained the honor of the entire family. Still, Leonato's attack upon his daughter is shocking to witness, and we are grateful that Friar Francis and Benedick are able to calm his rage.

By the time we see him again in Act 5 scene 1, he has obviously had time to think things through and has accepted the observations of Friar Francis, Benedick, and Beatrice that Hero has been wronged. We now see him attempting to defend his family name and honor against Don Pedro and Claudio's attack. Don Pedro and Claudio deliver the unkindest cut of all—they refuse to consider him worth fighting. They have not only stained his honor, but stripped him of it by telling him that he is too old and no longer of any consequence. This is the low point for Leonato. The code of ethics that he has spent his life believing in has deserted him at the very moment that he needs it most.

When the truth about Hero's innocence is finally revealed, we see that Leonato is truly a magnanimous man. When Claudio offers to submit to any punishment he can devise, what does he do? He sets up a series of tasks for him to complete to test the sincerity of Claudio's repentance and his worthiness to marry Hero.

Leonato has thereby ensured a successful resolution to the play and has a good time in the process. His lack of vindictiveness shows him to be a man of honor and good will.

## HERO

Hero is a typical young lady of the time. She is the daughter of a wealthy family, demure and well-brought up. We learn from Benedick's description of her that she is short, slight in stature with dark hair and dark eyes, and, even the cynical Benedick must admit, she is attractive.

When Don Pedro encounters Hero in the first scene, he says to Leonato, "I think this is your daughter." This implies that he has not seen her for awhile and that (as Don John will later note) Hero has turned into a "very forward March-chick" (meaning, "quite a dish") since he last laid eyes on her. Don Pedro will also refer to Hero as "very well worthy" meaning that her reputation is unassailable.

Hero barely utters a word in the first scene. This is partly because proper young ladies would not chatter on when gentlemen are conversing, but also because it would be nearly impossible for anyone to get a word in when Beatrice is present.

Hero most definitely plays second fiddle to her cousin Beatrice. In social situations, Beatrice dominates. But Hero loves her older cousin and, as we will see, respects her opinions.

In Act 2 scene 1, Beatrice, while acknowledging that Hero must obey her father's wishes in the choice of a husband, playfully advises her to make sure he is a handsome man or else say, "Father, as it please me."

Hero takes Beatrice's advice to heart. When the usually demure Hero dances with Don Pedro, she tells him that she will not agree to anything till she decides if she likes his looks. It is perhaps the joviality of a party, and the fact that they are both masked, that allows Hero to dare follow Beatrice's teachings and appear so brazen with the Prince.

Hero hardly speaks in the engagement scene. Beatrice reports her whispered message to Claudio that "he is in her heart," but other than that clue, we know nothing of what she feels. We have to assume that Hero is delighted to learn that the Prince was actually wooing her for Claudio's sake. Claudio is young, handsome, heroic, and no doubt exactly what she was wishing for in a husband.

It is finally in the Beatrice gulling scene that we get to learn something of Hero's personality. Here, she is in the presence of women and can be herself. Her first speech is full of her strategies for Beatrice's entrapment. She says that she will say "how Benedick is sick in love with Beatrice" and tells Ursula to praise Benedick "more than ever man did merit." But she then deviates somewhat from this plan, revealing to Beatrice all those things she has obviously thought but never dared say to her face—and all in the cause of helping her cousin to a good husband!

Hero obviously knows her cousin very well and chooses all the right things to say to hook her—calling her disdainful, criticizing her for valuing her wit so highly, claiming that she cannot love anyone else because she is too in love with herself, chastising Beatrice for her unfair treatment of men, and adding that she wouldn't dare tell Beatrice any of this because Beatrice would only make fun of her. Hero may appear to be shy and demure, but she shows herself here to be one smart cookie!

On the morning of her wedding, we see another side of Hero. As she and Margaret discuss her wedding gown, she says, "God give me joy to wear it, for my heart is exceeding heavy." This is an indication that she may be experiencing second thoughts about her marriage. This is not unusual for any young lady about to embark on a new phase of life. But for Hero, and indeed for many young ladies of her time whose marriages were arranged for them, it may be especially true. Hero is about to marry a man who she has only known for a week and to whom she has hardly spoken. She knows that all too often marriages of the upper classes were shallow affairs that had little to do with love, and Beatrice's earlier speech comparing marriage to the various dance steps of the time might well turn out to be true.

We next see Hero at the wedding. Here again, she is the perfect lady. When accused, she very simply attests to her innocence and makes no further explanations or excuses and then, with perfect daintiness, she faints. It is the sincerity and simplicity of Hero's responses that convince the friar that she lies "guiltless here under some biting error."

Hero is then kept out of sight until the situation is resolved. We have to wonder what Hero undergoes emotionally that allows her to be so gracious and magnanimous when we see her again in the last scene. What must Hero think of Claudio once the details of Don John's plot have been revealed? Whether she attributes his actions to the dictates of the honor code, or as symptoms of youthful folly and gullibility, we do not know, but in any case, Hero exhibits an incredible capacity for understanding and forgiveness.

When she and Claudio are reunited, it is the delicacy and gentleness of her words that give us hope that their marriage will not be like the ones Beatrice has referred to, but will grow into a strong and loving relationship.

## MARGARET

Margaret is about the same age as Hero, but having been born into a lower class family, she must work until she marries. She would then take care of her own household and children and be supported by her husband.

Margaret is Hero's waiting gentlewoman. This makes her one of the better placed servants in the household. Hers is a much less strenuous job than, say, the scullery maid's, who must scrub the pots and pans and keep the kitchen clean.

Margaret helps Hero to dress—no well-turned-out young lady of the time could possibly dress herself with all the hooks and laces that clothing of the day required. She also takes care of Hero's clothing, folding and storing it properly and sending things off to the housemaids when they need cleaning. She tends to Hero's personal belongings: keeping her perfume bottles filled, her hair brushes clean, and all the other very personal things a young lady might require. But her relationship with Hero and Beatrice often seems more like that of girlfriend than of servant.

We first hear her speak when she is dancing with Borachio after the banquet. Her appearance at the dance attests to her elevated position and of the casual atmosphere of Leonato's household. She and Borachio are clearly flirting with each other. Borachio will later tell Don John "how much [he is] in the favor of Margaret" and that he can get her to be a pawn in their plan to deceive Claudio and Don Pedro.

We must assume that Margaret was ignorant of the ramifications of her participation in Borachio's scheme. He probably asked her to arrange some ploy to get Hero and Beatrice out of their room, to then dress up in her mistress's gown, come to the window, and flirt with him as though they were a lord and lady. She, thinking it a harmless prank, willingly fulfills his fantasy, totally unaware of what the consequences might be.

In the scene when she is helping Hero to dress for her wedding, we see that Margaret goes far beyond the ordinary bounds of mistress/servant relationships in her dealings with both Hero and Beatrice. She jokes freely with Hero about her coming wedding night and even attempts to display her own witty prowess taking on the weakened-by-lovesickness Beatrice.

Margaret's light-heartedness in this scene further attests to the theory that she was ignorant of the malicious intent of her rendezvous at the window. Borachio's statement that she "knew not what she did when she spoke to me, but always hath been just and virtuous," gives further credence to this. We must wonder, though, how much Margaret learns of the details of Claudio's accusation against Hero. It seems unlikely that she could remain ignorant of what occurred at the wedding. Yet if she does know what happened, how could she keep from connecting it to her actions of the prior evening? This is a dilemma that Shakespeare leaves unanswered. It is up to the actress playing Margaret to determine what happens to her emotionally between the wedding and the public revelation of Hero's innocence. In any case, Margaret must be greatly relieved to have all things turn out so well in the end.

## ANTONIO

Antonio is Leonato's brother. He, like Leonato, is an "old man." Of course this is a relative term considering the youth of the other men in the play. He and Leonato could be in their fifties.

Antonio delightedly brings Leonato the news of the overheard conversation between Claudio and Don Pedro. He too must be excited at the prospect of his niece marrying into the royal family. In Act 2 scene 1, we note his slight apprehension about Beatrice's influence over Hero when he says, "Well niece, I trust you will be ruled by your father." He does not want Hero to follow Beatrice's example of being antimarriage.

It's not until Act 5 when he tries to calm his enraged brother's fury that we really get to see him in action. Realizing that Leonato will not be consoled, he encourages him to vent his anger upon those who deserve it and not upon himself.

When the Prince and Claudio come on, Leonato takes his brother's advice and turns his wrath toward

Claudio, challenging him to a duel. Antonio not only supports his brother's efforts, but gets so carried away in his own attack that Leonato is forced to try to calm him, giving this otherwise serious scene, a delightful comic twist.

**BORACHIO**

Borachio's name comes from a Spanish word for a wine container and quite obviously, Borachio at times holds far too much alcohol for his own good.

We meet him, though, in a sober state. He has been helping in the preparations for the big banquet at Leonato's and while "smoking a musty room" (burning incense or herbs to make the air smell fresh), he has overheard the Prince and Claudio talking.

He reports to Don John that he hid himself "behind the arras and there heard it agreed that the Prince should woo Hero, and having obtained her, give her to Count Claudio." This shows just how clever and resourceful Borachio is. Not only does he get the facts right, but he is smart enough to realize that this tidbit might be valuable ammunition for his master.

People with an affinity for malice attract others of similar nature, and so we have Don John, Conrade, and Borachio bonding together. While Borachio is certainly the smartest of this trio of malcontents, he is no happier with his social circumstances than is Don John or Conrade.

Borachio is probably the second or third son of a not-too-well-off family. He therefore has had to learn to live off his wits rather than off an inheritance, and his talents seem perfectly suited to serving Don John! Along with his cleverness, he must have a certain amount of charm, since Margaret is clearly fond of him.

By the time we see Borachio in Act 2 scene 2, he has devised the rather intricate plan that he hopes will bring joy to his master, by bringing misery to his master's nemesis. The fact that Don John pays well for such services—a thousand ducats in this case—obviously goes far to spark Borachio's imagination and initiative.

Having excessively celebrated the success of the charade, we next see the very drunken Borachio proudly confiding the details of it to Conrade. Overheard by the Watch, they are both arrested for this "most dangerous piece of lechery."

When the Prince finds himself at a loss to understand Dogberry's explanation for why Borachio and Conrade are bound, a sober and contrite Borachio confesses his part in the plot. Yet even here, facing certain punishment, we note Borachio's defiance of authority when he says, "What your wisdoms could not discover, these shallow fools have brought to light."

He shows himself to have certain redeeming qualities though, when he stands up like a man and takes full responsibility for his actions and refuses to let Margaret be blamed for any part in the scheme.

**CONRADE**

Conrade is probably the younger of Don John's followers. He appears to be less experienced and newer to the game than is Borachio. He also does not seem to know his master as well. Conrade attempts to give him advice about biding his time and being reasonable. Borachio knows that all Don John wants is revenge! But Conrade is a loyal follower, vowing "to the death, my lord" when Don John asks if they will assist him.

Conrade does not learn about the plot against Claudio until it has been executed—perhaps he's not as trusted as Borachio to take part in such exploits. His amazement that Borachio could have earned a thousand ducats for his undertaking is further proof that he hasn't been around for long.

Conrade might be a younger son of an elite family who, because of his past failures, is sent out to try to make it on his own and has hooked up with Don John in hopes of getting ahead without much effort.

He takes affront at Dogberry's calling him "sirrah" in Act 4 scene 2 claiming that he is "a gentleman" and displays a rather devil-may-care attitude when he calls Dogberry "an ass."

**FRIAR FRANCIS**

Friar Francis is a parish priest in Messina. He obviously knows Leonato and his family well. He is no doubt honored to be asked to perform the marriage ceremony for the Count and the governor's daughter—and with the Prince in attendance. He seems to be in fine good humor as he starts the ceremony.

As things start to fall apart, though, the friar remains silent. This is a very delicate situation for him. This is his Prince and a Count who are making these accusations; he knows he must step gingerly. The friar is a practical man and knows he must not risk offending the Prince. He therefore does not offer his opinions till the noble gentlemen depart.

We now see that he is a shrewd observer of human nature. He astutely assesses what has transpired, assuring Leonato that, in his best judgment, Hero is indeed guiltless and that "some biting error" has misled the Prince and Claudio.

While his observations are correct, the solution he offers is problematic. He suggests that the family put out the word that Hero is indeed dead.

The friar is a perceptive man though, who realizes that patience and circumspection will serve better than any thing else at this point. By proposing this lie, he also shows that he is not a stickler for the letter of church law and is willing to bend the truth in hopes of remedying the situation.

Claudio, of course, does not immediately mourn Hero's loss as the friar had predicted, but waits until her innocence is proved. The friar's plan did however allow the necessary time for things to eventually work themselves out. And had the friar not been able to calm Leonato, we have to wonder what Leonato might have done to poor Hero.

## URSULA

Ursula is another of Hero's waiting gentlewomen. She seems to be more mature than Margaret and is probably more content with her position. She is more servant and less girlfriend than Margaret.

She participates in Beatrice's gulling scene with the proper mixture of inquisitiveness and sincerity to help guarantee that Beatrice falls for the plot. She is loyal and competent and has no aspirations of climbing above her social circumstances.

## DOGBERRY

A "dogberry" can be a small shrub which bears tiny red berries or, employing the word's grosser imagery, it is another term for "doggie-doo"!

In *Much Ado*, Dogberry is the Master Constable of Messina. This means that he is in charge of keeping the peace in the town. Shakespeare's Dogberry and his team of bumbling assistants are the prototypes for numerous inept fictional policemen to follow—the Keystone Cops and Inspector Clouseau for example.

Dogberry is one of those Shakespearean characters whose ability to butcher the English language delightfully astounds us. Dogberry takes great pride in his language skills. In this sense, he is the lower-class parallel of Beatrice and Benedick. He too loves to hear himself talk. But, as opposed to the witty lovers who manipulate language to convey their points of view, Dogberry's great thrill is to impress others with what he considers his extensive vocabulary. Whenever possible, he will select a longer, more complicated word, and he will invariably distort it almost beyond recognition.

When we first meet Dogberry, he and his partner, Verges are instructing the team of watchmen who are to be on guard this night. Note that Dogberry probably does this every night, with every team of watchmen; he loves to demonstrate his importance.

The first order of business is to establish who should be the leader of the Watch. George Seacoal fits the bill because he can "write and read"–something Dogberry obviously admires.

Dogberry then proceeds to go over their orders. His instructions exemplify his peacekeeping policies: unless trouble comes and sits in your lap, don't interfere! This policy has probably worked well in Messina because the overall crime rate among the locals in this peaceful town is fairly low. But now strangers have come to town.

The Watch awakens Dogberry in the wee hours of the morning with the news of the arrests of Borachio and Conrade. Dogberry then heads over to Leonato's to inform him of what has happened. It's Dogberry's failure to inform Leonato of the importance of what has been discovered that allows Leonato to go to the church unprepared for what is to come.

The interrogation scene shows Dogberry to be the pompously inept bungler that he is. He is not only unable to elicit any pertinent information from Conrade and Borachio, but when the facts of the crime do become known, he completely misunderstands them.

But it is Dogberry's wonderfully puffed-up, indignant reaction to Conrade's calling him an ass that gives us the greatest insight into his character. Dogberry's immense ego has been injured. His response of total amazement that he, "a wise fellow . . . an officer . . . a householder; and which is more, as pretty a piece of flesh as any is in Messina" should be so insulted, is utterly sincere.

We last see Dogberry when, following the Sexton's instructions, he is bringing the prisoners to Leonato's. Here again, he demonstrates his lack of understanding of the true nature of the crime. It is only Borachio's confession that allows Don Pedro and Claudio to recognize the horrible error that they have committed.

But ultimately, whether he grasps the situation or not, it is Dogberry's dogged commitment to doing the right thing, that brings the offenses to light and saves the day, turning a potentially tragic outcome back to comedy.

## VERGES

Verges is Dogberry's assistant. He and Dogberry have probably been working together for a long time and they know each other very well. Verges is the perfect foil for Dogberry. He not only understands Dogberry, but has even learned over time to talk the same language.

Verges is the older of the two, and he seems perfectly happy to accept Dogberry's patronizing attitude toward him. His job is to support his Master Constable, and he is happy to serve in that capacity.

## THE WATCH

Shakespeare is a little vague about the nature of the Watch, but they are probably like our volunteer firemen. Most likely, they are local workmen who take turns serving as the night watchmen for the town.

The Second Watchman, named George Seacoal, can "write and read." This is quite a feat for someone of the lower classes of this time. Dogberry, in his usual bizarre manner, points this out.

The Watch are honest, sincere men who take their responsibility seriously. They also seem to be pretty bright; note how quickly they pick up on "Dogberryisms."

## SEXTON

A sexton is a church employee. He's usually the person who takes care of the church grounds, rings the church bells, and digs the graves. The Sexton in Messina can write, and that's why Dogberry sends for him when he is to examine the prisoners. He wants a written record of the proceedings.

Fortunately, the Sexton also turns out to be pretty savvy when it comes to conducting an interrogation. If it were not for his suggestions, Dogberry's questioning could have gone on forever. Benedick might have been dueling with Claudio by the time Dogberry got anything pertinent out of the prisoners.

## MESSENGER

The Messenger is an up-and-coming young soldier in Don Pedro's army. He has been sent ahead to signal the arrival of the Prince. He is quite overwhelmed by Beatrice. He has no doubt never been in the presence of such a young woman. It is to his credit that he emerges relatively unscathed from their encounter.

## BEATRICE AND BENEDICK

Beatrice and Benedick share many characteristics. Let's briefly look at some of the driving forces that propel both of them through the play before we examine them individually.

They are both pleasant and successful human beings who are appreciated by those around them, but they seem doomed to single life when we first meet them. Whether this is due to their aversion to falling in line with the social order of the time, or their reluctance to surrender a part of themselves by falling in love, we don't know yet, but they have nevertheless firmly established themselves as a merry sparring duo, and everyone has come to expect them to act as such whenever they meet.

Benedick is a confirmed bachelor who claims to distrust women. He tells us that while he is "loved of all ladies," he remains a "professed tyrant to their sex." He is well aware of the threat of cuckoldry that looms over a man if he gives himself to a wife. Benedick is not about to tempt fate by marrying. Beatrice says flat out that she "could not endure a husband!" She believes that marriage and repentance go hand in hand. These, at least, are their public justifications for remaining single. But perhaps there is more to this than meets the eye.

To fall in love, one has to surrender part of oneself to another and open one's heart to the possibility of pain. As brave as Benedick is in battle, and as brazen as Beatrice tries to make us believe she is, they are both clearly afraid to do this. It would make them vulnerable. A scary prospect for these two.

By the time we meet them, Beatrice and Benedick have become well-armored knights in their battle of wits. They only raise their visors to exchange verbal salvos on the battlefield. Their hearts are seemingly well protected inside their extensive armor. Wit is a weapon though—it can cut deeply. In the hands of the quick-witted, the cut can be devastating. The amount of pain that they have inflicted on each other by the time we encounter them seems impossible to heal.

And yet Beatrice and Benedick have no other opponents—no one else is a worthy challenger for either. They need each other; they compliment each other; they satisfy each other. Still, they frighten each other, because they know that to be together they would have to yield to each other, and neither will be the first one to blink—their guard is always up.

It is wonderfully ironic that these two characters who have become so entrapped in their personal avowals of independence can only find the freedom to admit their love for one another through the further entrapment of their respective gulling scenes.

## BEATRICE

Beatrice is certainly one of Shakespeare's most fascinating and original characters. She is witty, intelligent, strong-willed, and extremely independent—and she is a woman!

Beatrice is an orphan and probably hasn't any inherited fortune. It is this absence of wealth that allows her much of the freedom she enjoys. Were she an heiress, there would be tremendous pressure on her to marry someone with whom she could combine fortunes. So, in some cases, it pays to be poor!

Beatrice lives with her Uncle Leonato, the governor of Messina, and his daughter, Hero. Let's track Beatrice through the play and see what we can learn about her.

We meet Beatrice in the first scene. A messenger has come to announce the return of the triumphant soldiers from the wars. Beatrice jumps into the conversation to ask about "Signior Mountanto." She is, of course, referring to Benedick. A *mountanto* is an upward thrust in fencing terminology. Here we see not only her desire to find out whether Benedick has returned unscathed, but also note the rather blatant sexual innuendo of her inquiry.

The Messenger is somewhat taken aback by this very unique lady. She conducts herself as a man might;

taking focus and speaking freely. The Messenger is certainly not used to such conduct in a woman.

Leonato tells the Messenger that Beatrice's behavior is the result of a "merry war betwixt Signior Benedick and her" and that "they never meet but there's a skirmish of wit between them." Beatrice takes great pride in pointing out that Benedick is the loser whenever they engage in their battles of wit.

As this scene progresses, Beatrice shows herself to be a self-assured, highly intelligent, and somewhat aggressive female. But as we shall see, combined with these characteristics is a gaiety and charm, along with a deeply compassionate nature, that draws people to her and makes them adore her.

Once Beatrice has brought up Benedick's name, the conversation becomes dominated by her putdowns of him, until he finally appears. When Benedick takes no notice of Beatrice (no doubt intentionally), Beatrice makes a point of attracting his attention with, "I wonder that you will still be talking, Signior Benedick, nobody marks you." Even if nobody else was taking note of Benedick, Beatrice was certainly hanging on his every word!

Now the fun begins. We have our two great wits face-to-face and barb-to-barb ready for action, and they hardly ever miss a beat. The first thing that Beatrice and Benedick do when they encounter each other, is to let the other know that neither has become involved with anyone else since they last met. Benedick makes the point by saying that while he is "loved of all ladies" except, of course, Beatrice, he himself is in love with none. Beatrice responds by pointing out that she is of the same mind, and that she would "rather hear [her] dog bark at a crow than a man swear he loves" her. Odd that these two who protest to have no interest in each other, should start off by establishing their availability! They then proceed to insult one another until Benedick ends the conversation, leaving Beatrice somewhat frustrated.

We next encounter Beatrice talking with her family the evening of the banquet. They are discussing Don John. Beatrice again takes the opportunity to bring the conversation round to Benedick. We clearly see that he is always very prominent in her thoughts.

Here, as in the first scene of the play, Beatrice monopolizes her social scene, just as we'll see Benedick does his. She goes off on riffs whenever it strikes her fancy. She obviously loves to hear herself talk and enjoys manipulating language.

Beatrice's skill with language may have a purpose other than mere entertainment; she seems to use her wit and words to protect herself and avoid intimacy, thereby establishing an emotional distance between herself and others.

This becomes more obvious with the discussion of marriage. Beatrice's aversion to the institution becomes apparent as the scene progresses. Elizabethan marriages were usually one-sided affairs. The wife was expected to be totally subservient to her husband and forfeit any independence she may have enjoyed. Beatrice is certainly not about to do this for anyone.

Beatrice's speech comparing the stages of marriage to various dance styles of the time is very telling indeed. Beatrice has obviously observed that many marriages are not happy unions and that "repentance" is too often the end result of them. Although she knows that Hero must follow Leonato's wishes regarding her matrimonial future, Beatrice is quick to advise her to make sure that the prospective man is pleasing to her, or else she should object to the match.

It's interesting to note that even Leonato seems to agree with Beatrice's assessment of marriage with his line, "Cousin, you apprehend passing shrewdly." One wonders what his married life was like!

Later in the scene, when Beatrice and Benedick are dancing together, we have to assume that they recognize each other—why else would they make such a point of attacking one another? When Benedick belittles Beatrice's wit (her most prized attribute), she comes back at him with a most penetrating attack calling him a "dull fool"! She's got him—where it hurts—and she knows it!

When Beatrice brings Claudio to Don Pedro, she is in excellent good spirits because of her recent victory over Benedick. It is here that Beatrice gives us a glimmer of insight into her relationship with Benedick. When Don Pedro says to her, "Come, lady, come; you have lost the heart of Signior Benedick," Beatrice responds with, "Indeed, my lord, he lent it me awhile, and I gave him use for it—a double heart for his single one. Marry, once before he won it with false dice, therefore your grace may well say I have lost it." Beatrice has obviously opened her heart to Benedick in the past, and he hurt her deeply. She is not about to let this happen again.

This explains a great deal about Beatrice. Perhaps her bravado about men and marriage is merely a cover to conceal her pain. She has become so proficient at this that she has even managed to deceive herself.

Once the alliance between Hero and Claudio is established, Beatrice, half jokingly, refers to her own state of singleness. Don Pedro picks up on this and, in the same light-hearted vein, offers to get Beatrice a husband. When Beatrice pushes the game further saying that she would rather have one *begot* by Don Pedro's father; Don Pedro offers himself. Beatrice has perhaps stepped in a little too deeply, and she must find a graceful way out. She proceeds to try to do this by flattering Don Pedro.

But by this time, Don Pedro clearly understands

where Beatrice's heart is engaged, even if she will not admit it to herself. When Beatrice departs, Don Pedro suggests to the others that they try to bring Beatrice and Benedick together. It is interesting to note that while Beatrice and Benedick may have deceived themselves about their feelings for each other, everyone else seems to recognize what's going on.

Beatrice next appears when she is sent to call Benedick in to dinner. He, by now, has been transformed by his gulling scene into a lover, but Beatrice is still looking through the eyes of a cynic and is somewhat puzzled by Benedick's out-of-character responses to her. When his usually witty retorts don't materialize, she is left with nothing to say and departs.

But then comes her gulling scene, and Beatrice listens, as her closest intimates reveal that Benedick loves her! They then proceed to catalog her shortcomings. What must Beatrice be thinking as Hero and her gentlewoman refer to her as disdainful, hardhearted, and self-centered, when they claim that she trivializes people's sincere emotions, and say that she is willing to wound others deeply for the glory of her own wit? How does Beatrice feel when she hears them say that they will advise Benedick to "fight against his passion"?

When they depart, we see a miraculous transformation in Beatrice. Her cynical cocoon drops away and Beatrice "the lover" is revealed. She vows to instantly surrender those traits that have garnered her such a reputation and says that she will act with such kindness that Benedick will be compelled to marry her! For, she says, she knows Benedick to be even more wonderful than has been reported.

In Act 3 scene 4 we see Beatrice in the throes of lovesickness. Imagine the night she has spent—going over every word she overheard in the orchard, reliving her past encounters with Benedick, realizing how very much in love with him she is, and fearing that she may have been too snide in the past. She has probably not slept a wink. She is bleary-eyed and confused and definitely lovesick.

When Beatrice enters Hero's room in Act 3 scene 4, her defenses are down. She is in a weakened state—she seems to be suffering from some sort of sickness. We know it's love!

Beatrice sees Benedick for the first time since her gulling scene at Hero's wedding. All the feelings that have been raging in her heart come to the fore. But as these thoughts race through her head, she begins to take note of the strange events that are taking place before her eyes. Claudio is rejecting her cousin in the most vicious manner, accusing her of being a loose woman, a slut! This is unbelievable!

When Hero collapses, Beatrice seems to be the only person willing to stand up for her. She has not one moment's doubt about her cousin's innocence. Yet, this woman who is usually so quick witted, who always seems to have something to say about everything, can mutter little more than "no" when she is asked if she spent the night in Hero's room.

Beatrice, who earlier in the play had claimed that her "merry heart [kept her] on the windy side of care," no longer is able to cut herself off from her feelings. Her emotions, which have always before been tempered by her rational self, are now out there—raw and immediate.

When Beatrice and Benedick are left alone in the church, we see Beatrice reduced to tears. Beatrice now feels the harsh frustrations of Elizabethan womanhood. Not her quick wit, nor her daring, nor her sharp tongue can do anything to help restore her cousin's lost honor—and without honor, Beatrice knows that Hero is doomed. Beatrice herself is helpless; she is merely a woman; she can only weep.

Beatrice's passionate desire to avenge her cousin's honor, along with her own newly acknowledged deep love for Benedick, have become inexorably intertwined. At this heightened emotional moment—with Beatrice's heart so full of love for Benedick that there is no part "left to protest," along with the utter disdain she feels for Claudio, the "villain that hath slandered, scorned, dishonored" her cousin—Beatrice responds with raw emotional honesty to Benedick's request, "Come, bid me do anything for thee" with the two most shocking words of the play, "Kill Claudio!"

When Benedick replies, "Not for the wide world!" Beatrice is distraught. She not only feels anguish for her cousin, but also rejection from her supposed best friend and avowed lover. She is disgusted with men and her speech about manhood expresses her disdain for them. It is a great relief for Beatrice when Benedick finally agrees to challenge Claudio.

We must assume that Beatrice spends the interim between the wedding and the time when Benedick returns to her comforting Hero and reassuring Leonato of Hero's innocence. But this is also a time when she must be reflecting on her feelings for Benedick. By taking up her challenge, he has proven his love for her, and now Beatrice must be extremely concerned for his safety. Surely Benedick is the superior soldier, but dueling is a dangerous business and anything could happen. Beatrice is no doubt greatly relieved when Margaret comes to tell her that Benedick is waiting for her.

When she sees him, she tries hard to be the proper lady, responding to his "wouldst thou come when I called thee?" with a demure, "Yea, signior, and depart when you bid me." But she just can't keep it up and quickly reverts to her own witty self.

In the last scene, we see Beatrice and Benedick,

confident in their love for each other, having a perfectly delightful time exhibiting their witty by-play at their friends' expense. Theirs will be the sort of marriage that Shakespeare seems to be calling for in *Much Ado*—a marriage founded on love, equality, and mutual respect and tempered with reason.

## BENEDICK

Don Pedro describes Benedick's attributes as follows, "he is of a noble strain, of approved valor and confirmed honesty." Let's look at each of these in turn and see what they meant to someone of the 16th century.

*Of noble strain* This meant that Benedick was born into a noble family. Europe of this era was a class-structured society and to be born into the nobility was a huge advantage. It meant that you had land, money, education, leisure, invitations to all the best parties, and, perhaps (most important of all), you had honor. The only disadvantages to the circumstances of Benedick's birth was that he was not the first-born son. If he had been, he would have inherited the family lands and titles and be running the estate (or be home learning the ropes, if his father were still alive). Younger sons had relatively few options. Since they were noble, working for a living was out of the question. So what is a noble body to do? Generally, there were four choices:

1. Stay home and help run the estate (assuming you were on good terms with your oldest brother).
2. Go into the church at some fairly high level.
3. Attach yourself to some other powerful lord and become one of his attendants.
4. Join the army!

This last option was popular because most aristocrats were trained from an early age in the arts of war. Benedick chose numbers 3 and 4, attaching himself to the Prince of Aragon as a soldier. When we meet Benedick in *Much Ado* he has become one of Don Pedro's closest confidantes.

*Of approved valor* The quickest way to prove (and improve) one's honor was on the battlefield. A good soldier was highly valued by kings and feudal lords alike. Courage in battle was the first mark of honor (after status of birth). A young nobleman who distinguished himself in battle usually rose rapidly in esteem and in position. Benedick has done just that.

*Confirmed honesty* A man who is honest can be counted on. He can be believed. His prince can turn his back on him without fear. Feudalism is based on pledges of trust and loyalty. This was the basic fabric which held society together. The loss of honor due to treachery damned a man completely; even the opposing side, which may have gained from a man's treachery, would never trust him. Benedick proves his honesty more than once during the course of the play.

These three attributes assure Benedick of a continuing favorable place in Don Pedro's (his liege lord's) domain. But these traits belonged to many nobles of the time. What sets Benedick apart from your average aristocrat and makes him one of Shakespeare's most delightful creations?

Benedick is somewhat at odds with his society. He, like Beatrice, is untraditional: neither has bought completely into the accepted thinking of their time; they are not slaves to convention. This allows them to hold and express some very original points of view.

Benedick has a quick wit. He is very perceptive—it is hard to pull the wool over his eyes, except perhaps where Beatrice is concerned. Most important of all, he is a reasonable man. Let's follow him through the play and see what more we can learn about him.

At the top of the play we see his wit displayed with Beatrice, and again with Don Pedro and Claudio. We see that he can go too far. Don Pedro has to send him away just to be able to get a word in with Claudio.

During the party scene, Benedick exhibits two more facets of his character. He is extremely sensitive when it comes to Beatrice. His soliloquy after Beatrice has lacerated him during the dance is a marvelous example of a man trying to stitch himself back together. Benedick is vulnerable to Beatrice's criticism because he cares so very much about what she thinks of him. Note too that it is Benedick who, while lambasting Beatrice to Don Pedro in Act 2 scene 1, brings up the subject of marriage, "I would not marry her though she were endowed with all that Adam had left him before he transgressed." Interesting—no one had mentioned the idea of him marrying Beatrice! What's on his mind?

Benedick also demonstrates his honesty by daring to express his disapproval when he believes Don Pedro has wooed Hero for himself. This is a man who speaks his mind.

The speeches which precede and follow his gulling scene, beautifully portray how love changes everything. Before he hears that Beatrice loves him, he presents an air-tight case why he should not get married. Afterwards, he says he never thought it would happen, but since it has, he can't wait to jump smack-dab in the middle. He says, "Happy are they that can hear their detractions and can put them to mending." From that moment on, he transforms from "tyrant to their sex" to being "horribly in love." His journey has only just begun.

We next see him exhibiting all the signs of the conventional lover. He is wearing cologne, he sighs, he seems sad. He is suffering love, and loving every minute of it.

In the wedding scene, his perceptiveness and reasonableness come to the fore. He figures out who the villain is. He keeps his head while everyone around him goes ballistic. He attempts to reason with Beatrice. Yet, he winds up challenging his best friend. So why does he do it? Is he a fool for love?

Benedick doesn't just go with the flow here. He weighs the options. He is sure that he loves Beatrice. He has known it for a long time. He just hasn't dared admit it. He believes that Beatrice loves him. He also understands what Beatrice is talking about. Claudio may or may not have been deceived, but he has made a villain of himself by acting in such a mean-spirited way. It is at this point that we see reason and passion standing toe to toe, and Benedick realizes that, in this case, reason must surrender to passion.

Both Benedick and Leonato voice their sentiments about the inability to experience another's pain over the course of the play. Leonato says, "Men can counsel and speak comfort to that grief which they themselves not feel," and Benedick says, "everyone can master a grief but he that has it." The fact is, it is almost impossible to experience pain as acutely as the one who is aching. But Benedick does this. He does it by being so much in love, that his heart is wide open and perfectly attuned to Beatrice's. His love allows him to feel her passion and her fury. His empathy will allow him to act on Hero and Beatrice's behalf because he is now truly connected to Beatrice's feelings. This is what love is really all about.

Benedick comes to the conclusion that to be truly honorable in this situation, honor must be used to serve love. Benedick must challenge Claudio. Imagine though, how he must feel as he goes to do it. He realizes that in challenging Claudio, he must also part company with Don Pedro, who obviously shares Claudio's point of view. This is a very serious matter. He knows that they are not entirely to blame. He also suspects that with a little inquiry into the matter things could probably be cleared up. But he is committed.

As he is going, though, the gods of comedy are contriving to save the day, and we realize that things will work out well. Whew!

Benedick returns to Beatrice to report his completion of the challenge. As they talk, he begins to realize that he and Beatrice are not suited for the customary ways of courtship—no poetry and no singing of love songs. He will show love in his own way. What that is is not clear just yet. But between them, he and Beatrice will discover it.

In the last scene, Beatrice and Benedick are becoming a team. They are now acting in unison in their dealings with the others. This does not mean that, have lost their individuality, but that they have surrendered enough of it to the other to be able to act in concert. They now compliment and reinforce each other. Both say that they love the other "no more than reason." Reason will be their referee, hopefully it will guide them and keep them playing fair in this game of love.

# Much Ado About Nothing

## CAST LIST

| | |
|---|---|
| DON PEDRO, Prince of Aragon | DP |
| BENEDICK, a young lord from Padua | Ben |
| CLAUDIO, a young lord from Florence | Cl |
| LEONATO, Governor of Messina | Leo |
| ANTONIO, brother of Leonato | Ant |
| DON JOHN, bastard brother of Don Pedro | DJ |
| BORACHIO } Don John's men | Bor |
| CONRADE | Con |
| DOGBERRY, master constable | Dog |
| VERGES, assistant to Dogberry | Ver |
| FIRST WATCH, officers working for Dogberry | W1 |
| SECOND WATCH, | W2 |
| FRIAR FRANCIS, a priest | FF |
| SEXTON, an employee of the church | Sext |
| MESSENGER, young officer of Don Pedro's | Mess |
| BEATRICE, niece of Leonato | Bea |
| HERO, daughter of Leonato | Her |
| MARGARET } Hero's waiting gentlewomen | Mar |
| URSULA | Ur |

*Listed on the right are abbreviations of the characters' names used in the stage directions. Refer to Glossary on page 167 for explanation of other abbreviations used.*

*Within the stage directions an asterisk ( * ) indicates a suggestion to see the chapter on acting techniques and theatrical conventions.*

*Bracketed notations ( [ ] ) that appear throughout the text are interpretive hints that we've included for actors doing either a reading or a production of the play.*

*Note that the stage directions included indicate relative spatial relationships and will have to be adapted to the actual playing space that you are working on.*

## Act One · Scene 1        scene analysis

*Much Ado* opens with Leonato reading a letter that tells him of Don Pedro's arrival that evening into Messina. We learn that Don Pedro and his men are returning victorious from a war. We also hear mention of a young man from Florence named Claudio who has covered himself with glory in the wars.

Beatrice, Leonato's niece, asks the Messenger about a gentleman whom she refers to as "Signior Mountanto." Hero, Leonato's daughter, explains that Beatrice is referring to Signior Benedick. The Messenger tells Beatrice that Signior Benedick has returned from the wars in the same good humor as when he departed. Beatrice then proceeds to verbally put Signior Benedick down. Leonato explains that Beatrice and Benedick have a history of warring wits.

At this point, Don Pedro, Claudio, Benedick, and Don John arrive on the scene. Pleasantries are exchanged followed by a "skirmish of wit" between Beatrice and Benedick.

We then learn that Leonato has invited the Prince and his entourage to remain in Messina as his guests. All exit leaving Benedick and Claudio. Claudio reveals his infatuation with Hero to Benedick, and Benedick, the "professed tyrant" to the female sex, expresses his disappointment in Claudio's decision to "turn husband."

Don Pedro reenters to find out what has kept his friends. Benedick reveals the news that Claudio is in love. After some friendly banter about Benedick's aversion to marriage, Don Pedro sends Benedick off on an errand.

Claudio inquires about Hero's status and discovers that she is Leonato's only heir. Don Pedro then offers to assist Claudio in obtaining Hero for his wife.

## Act One · Scene 1        vernacular

*[enter Leonato, Hero, Beatrice & Messenger]*
LEONATO: *[reading letter]*
I learn from this letter that Don Pedro of Aragon is coming tonight to Messina.

MESSENGER:
He is very close by. He was only three miles away when I left him.

LEONATO:
How many gentlemen did you lose in this battle?

MESSENGER:
Only a few—and no one of note.

LEONATO:
A victory is twice as good when the winning side comes home unscathed. I read here that Don Pedro has heaped high praise on a young man from Florence named Claudio.

MESSENGER:
Very well deserved on his part. He has conducted himself beyond what one expects of someone so young. Looking like a lamb, but performing the feats of a lion.

BEATRICE:
I wonder, is Monsieur Magnifico returned from the wars or not?

MESSENGER:
I don't know anyone with that name, lady.

HERO:
My cousin means Signior Benedick from Padua.

MESSENGER:
Oh, he's returned and is as pleasant as ever—and he's a good soldier too, lady.

BEATRICE:
And he's a good soldier compared to a lady—but how is he compared to a lord?

| Act One·Scene 1 **original abridged** | Act One·Scene 1 **stage directions** |
|---|---|

*[enter Leonato, Hero, Beatrice & Messenger]*
LEONATO: *[reading letter]*
I learn in this letter that Don Pedro of
Aragon comes this night to Messina.

*(enter UC, Leo & Mess, Mess
L of Leo, followed by Bea &
Her, Her L of Bea, Leo & Mess
X RC, Bea & Her stop UC)*

MESSENGER:
He is very near. He was not three
leagues off when I left him.

LEONATO:
How many gentlemen have you lost in this
action?

MESSENGER:
But few—and none of name.

LEONATO:
A victory is twice itself when the
achiever brings home full numbers. I
find here that Don Pedro hath bestowed
much honor on a young Florentine called
Claudio.

MESSENGER:
Much deserved on his part. He hath borne
himself beyond the promise of his age,
doing in the figure of a lamb, the feats
of a lion.

BEATRICE:
I pray you, is Signior Mountanto returned
from the wars or no?

*(X to L of Mess)*

MESSENGER:
I know none of that name, lady.

HERO:
My cousin means Signior Benedick of Padua.

*(X C)*

MESSENGER:
O, he's returned and as pleasant as ever—
and a good soldier too, lady.

BEATRICE:
And a good soldier to a lady—but what is
he to a lord?

MESSENGER:
He's a lord compared to a lord, a man to
a man—full of honorable virtues.

BEATRICE:
It's true. He's full of it! But what's
he full of?—well we are all human.

LEONATO:
You musn't, sir, misunderstand my niece.
There is a kind of merry war between Signior
Benedick and her. They can never meet with-
out a skirmish of wit between them.

BEATRICE:
Alas, he never wins any. In our last
conflict, four of his five wits went
hobbling away, so now he's only left with
one! Who is his latest companion? Every
month he has a new best friend.

MESSENGER:
Is that possible.

BEATRICE:
Easily possible—his faithfulness is
like the fashion of hats, it's always
changing.

MESSENGER:
I see, lady, that the gentleman is not counted
among your friends.

BEATRICE:
No—and if he were, I'd demand a recount.
But I beg you, who is his latest companion.
Is there no young tough who would dare to
go to the devil with him?

MESSENGER:
He is seen most in the company of the very
noble Claudio.

MESSENGER:
A lord to a lord, a man to a man—stuffed
with all honorable virtues.

BEATRICE:
It is so indeed. He is no less than a
stuffed man! But for the stuffing—well
we are all mortal.

*(Bea X to Her, Bea, Her & Leo laugh at this)*

LEONATO:
You must not, sir, mistake my niece.
There is a kind of merry war betwixt Signior
Benedick and her. They never meet but
there's a skirmish of wit between them.

*(Bea turns back to listen)*

BEATRICE:
Alas, he gets nothing by that. In our last
conflict four of his five wits went
halting off, and now is the whole man
governed with one! Who is his companion
now? He hath every month a new sworn
brother.

MESSENGER:
Is't possible?

BEATRICE:
Very easily possible—he wears his faith
but as the fashion of his hat, it ever
changes.

*(Bea & Her laugh at this)*

MESSENGER:
I see, lady, the gentleman is not in your
books.

BEATRICE:
No—an he were, I would burn my study.
But I pray you, who is his companion? Is
there no young squarer will make a voyage
with him to the devil?

*(Xing to Mess)*

MESSENGER:
He is most in the company of the right
noble Claudio.

BEATRICE:
Oh Lord, he will attach himself like a leech—
he's more easily caught than the plague and
whoever gets him, instantly goes mad. God
help noble Claudio.

MESSENGER:
I will stay on your good side, lady.

BEATRICE:
Do good friend.

MESSENGER:
Don Pedro is here.

[enter Don Pedro, Claudio, Benedick,
Don John, Borachio & Conrade]
DON PEDRO:
Good Signior Leonato, have you come to
greet your trouble?

LEONATO:
Trouble never came to my house resembling
your honorable self. For when troubles are
gone, comfort should take its place; but
when you depart, sorrow remains and
happiness bids farewell.

DON PEDRO:
You take on your burdens too willingly.
I believe this is your daughter.

LEONATO:
Her mother has often told me so.

BENEDICK:
Were you in doubt sir, that you asked her?

LEONATO:
Signior Benedick, no—for then you were
a mere child.

DON PEDRO:
I think you are answered, Benedick.

BEATRICE:
O Lord, he will hang upon him like a disease—he is sooner caught than the pestilence—and the taker runs presently mad. God help the noble Claudio!

MESSENGER:
I will hold friends with you, lady.

BEATRICE:
Do, good friend.

MESSENGER:
Don Pedro is approached.

[enter Don Pedro, Claudio, Benedick, Don John, Borachio & Conrade]
DON PEDRO:
Good Signior Leonato, are you come to meet your trouble?

LEONATO:
Never came trouble to my house in the likeness of your Grace, for trouble being gone, comfort should remain; but when you depart, sorrow abides and happiness takes his leave.

DON PEDRO:
You embrace your charge too willingly. I think this is your daughter.

LEONATO:
Her mother hath many times told me so.

BENEDICK:
Were you in doubt sir, that you asked her?

LEONATO:
Signior Benedick, no—for then were you a child.

DON PEDRO:
You have it full, Benedick.

(Bea puts her arm around Mess' shoulder & brings him DRC)

(looking off DL)

(enter DL, DP X C, Her counter* R to Leo, Ben & Cl X DLC, DJ, Bor & Con stay DL)

(X C & bow* to DP)

(DP X to Her who curtsies*)

(X to L of DP)

BENEDICK:
If Signior Leonato is her father, she would
not have . . .

BEATRICE: *[interrupting]*
I wonder why you're still talking, Signior
Benedick—nobody's listening to you.

BENEDICK:
What, my dear Lady Disdain—are you still
living?

BEATRICE:
Is it possible that Disdain could die
while she has so fine an example as Signior
Benedick to pick on? Even Courtesy would
turn into disdain if you came anywhere near
her.

BENEDICK:
Then courtesy is a traitor. But I am
sure I am loved by all ladies—except
for you; and I wish I could find a soft
spot in my heart, for truly, I love
none.

BEATRICE:
You make women very happy—they would
otherwise have been bothered by a malicious
suitor. I thank God and my cold bloodedness,
that I am like you—I'd rather
hear my dog bark at a crow than a man
swear he loves me.

BENEDICK:
Let God forever keep your ladyship in that
frame of mind, so some gentleman or other
shall escape the inevitable scratched face.

BEATRICE:
Scratching couldn't make it any worse
if it were a face like yours.

BENEDICK:
I wish my horse were as fast as your
tongue and had such stamina. But you
keep right on going, by God, I'm done.

| Act One·Scene 1 **original abridged** | Act One·Scene 1 **stage directions** |
|---|---|

**BENEDICK:**
If Signior Leonato be her father, she would not have . . .

**BEATRICE:** *[interrupting]*
I wonder that you will still be talking, Signior Benedick—nobody marks you.

**BENEDICK:**
What, my dear Lady Disdain—are you yet living?

**BEATRICE:**
Is it possible Disdain should die while she hath such meet food to feed it as Signior Benedick? Courtesy itself must convert to disdain if you come in her presence.

*(Xing L a step, Her, Leo, DP, & Cl watch and laugh appropriately, Mess, DJ, Bor & Con watch in silence)*

**BENEDICK:**
Then is courtesy a turncoat. But it is certain I am loved of all ladies, only you excepted; and I would I could find it in my heart that I had not a hard heart, for truly I love none.

*(Xing R a step)*

**BEATRICE:**
A dear happiness to women—they would else have been troubled with a pernicious suitor. I thank God and my cold blood, I am of your humor for that—I had rather hear my dog bark at a crow than a man swear he loves me.

**BENEDICK:**
God keep your ladyship still in that mind, so some gentleman or other shall scape a predestinate scratched face.

*(Xing to Bea a step)*

**BEATRICE:**
Scratching could not make it worse, and 'twere such a face as yours were.

*(Xing to Ben a step)*

**BENEDICK:**
I would my horse had the speed of your tongue and so good a continuer. But keep your way, a God's name, I have done.

*(Bea and Ben are face to face)*

*(Ben X to Cl)*

BEATRICE:
You always end like a stubborn mule. I
know your tricks.

DON PEDRO:
Signior Claudio and Signior Benedick, my
dear friend Leonato has extended you an
invitation. I told him we'll stay at least
a month and he heartily hopes something will
detain us even longer.

LEONATO: *[to Don John]*
Let me bid you welcome, my lord. Since you
are reconciled with the Prince, your brother,
I offer you my respects.

DON JOHN:
I thank you. I'm not a man of many words,
but I thank you.

LEONATO:
Will it please your Grace to lead the way?

DON PEDRO:
Give me your hand, Leonato—we will go
together.
*[all exit except Benedick & Claudio]*

CLAUDIO:
Benedick, did you take note of Signior
Leonato's daughter?

BENEDICK:
I didn't take note of her—but I did see her.

CLAUDIO:
Isn't she a proper young lady?

BENEDICK:
Do you want my honest frank opinion?
Or do you want me to speak in my usual
manner—as a well-known detractor of
their sex?

CLAUDIO:
No, I beg you to speak seriously.

BEATRICE:
You always end with a jade's trick. I
know you of old.

*(X to R of Her)*

DON PEDRO:
Signior Claudio and Signior Benedick, my
dear friend Leonato hath invited you all.
I tell him we shall stay here at least a
month, and he heartily prays some occasion
may detain us longer.

*(DP & Leo X to Ben & Cl)*

LEONATO: *[to Don John]*
Let me bid you welcome, my lord. Being
reconciled to the Prince your brother,
I owe you all duty.

*(Xing DS, looking DL at DJ)*

*(Leo bows to DJ)*

DON JOHN:
I thank you. I am not of many words but I
thank you.

*(taking a step R towards Leo)*

LEONATO:
Please it your Grace lead on?

*(turning to DP)*

DON PEDRO:
Your hand, Leonato—we will go together.
*[all exit except Benedick & Claudio]*

*(taking Leo's arm, exit UC,
DJ, Bor, Con & Mess follow,
Bea, Her, Ben, Cl, meet UC,
Ben & Cl bow to ladies, Bea
& Her curtsy & exit UC, Cl
brings Ben C)*

CLAUDIO:
Benedick, didst thou note the daughter
of Signior Leonato?

BENEDICK:
I noted her not—but I looked on her.

CLAUDIO:
Is she not a modest young lady?

BENEDICK:
Do you question me for my simple true
judgment? Or would you have me speak
after my custom—as a professed tyrant
to their sex?

CLAUDIO:
No, I pray thee speak in sober judgment.

BENEDICK:
Why truly—I think she's too short for
high praise, too tawny for fair praise,
and too tiny for a great praise. I can
only pay her this compliment, if she
were other than she is, she'd not be
pretty, and since she is what she is, I
don't like her.

CLAUDIO:
You think I'm kidding. I really want you
to tell me how you like her.

BENEDICK:
Are you looking to buy her that you're asking
about her?

CLAUDIO:
Could anyone buy such a jewel?

BENEDICK:
Yes, and a case to keep her in. But are you
asking this seriously? Come on, how am I
to take you?

CLAUDIO:
To my eye she is the sweetest lady that
I have ever seen.

BENEDICK:
I can still see without spectacles, and I
see no such thing. There's her cousin—if
she weren't possessed by a she-devil—
exceeds her in beauty as a May day does
a December frost. But I hope you don't
intend to become a husband, do you?

CLAUDIO:
I would, even if I'd sworn not to, if Hero
would be my wife.

BENEDICK:
Has it come to this? Honestly, isn't there
one man in the world who will not be made
a fool? Will I never see a sixty-year-old
bachelor again? Oh well! Look, Don Pedro
has come back for you.

BENEDICK:
Why, i' faith, methinks she's too low
for a high praise, too brown for a fair
praise, too little for a great praise.
Only this commendation I can afford her,
that were she other than she is, she were
unhandsome, and being no other but as she
is, I do not like her.

CLAUDIO:
Thou thinkest I am in sport. I pray thee
tell me truly how thou likest her.

BENEDICK:
Would you buy her, that you inquire after
her?

CLAUDIO:
Can the world buy such a jewel?

BENEDICK:
Yea, and a case to put it into. But speak
you this with a sad brow? Come, in what
key shall a man take you?

CLAUDIO:
In mine eye she is the sweetest lady that
ever I looked on.

BENEDICK:
I can see yet without spectacles, and I
see no such matter. There's her cousin,
and she were not possessed with a fury,
exceeds her in beauty as the first of May
doth the last of December. But I hope you
have no intent to turn husband, have you?

CLAUDIO:
I would, though I had sworn the contrary,
if Hero would be my wife.

BENEDICK:
Is't come to this? In faith, hath not the
world one man but he will wear his cap
with suspicion? Shall I never see a
bachelor of threescore again? Go to!
Look, Don Pedro is returned to seek you.

*(Ben bring Cl DC, arm on Cl's shoulder)*

*(X R & sit DS end of bench)*

*(X to US end of bench)*

*(putting his foot up on bench, leaning arm on knee)*

*(mussing Cl's hair then Xing DLC)*

*(turning back to Cl, sees DP)*

*[enter Don Pedro]*
DON PEDRO:
What's kept you here, that you didn't come to Leonato's?

BENEDICK:
I wish your Grace would force me to tell.

DON PEDRO:
I order you on your allegiance.

BENEDICK:
Your hear that, Count Claudio. I can keep a secret as well as a mute; but on my allegiance—you hear that—on my allegiance! He's in love. With who? Note how short his answer is—with Hero, Leonato's short daughter.

DON PEDRO:
The lady is certainly worthy.

CLAUDIO:
You're saying that to lead me on, my lord.

DON PEDRO:
Truly, I'm just saying what I think.

CLAUDIO:
Honestly, my lord, I'm just saying what I think.

BENEDICK:
And by my two 'trulys' and 'honestlys,' my lord, I'm just saying what I think.

CLAUDIO:
That I love her, I feel.

DON PEDRO:
That she is worthy, I know.

BENEDICK:
That I neither feel she should be loved, nor know she should be worthy, is the

*[enter Don Pedro]*

DON PEDRO:
What hath held you here, that you
followed not to Leonato's?

BENEDICK:
I would your Grace would constrain me
to tell.

DON PEDRO:
I charge thee on thy allegiance.

BENEDICK:
You hear, Count Claudio. I can be as
secret as a dumb man; but on my
allegiance—mark you this—on my
allegiance! He is in love. With who?
Mark how short his answer is—with
Hero, Leonato's short daughter.

DON PEDRO:
The lady is very well worthy.

CLAUDIO:
You speak this to fetch me in, my lord.

DON PEDRO:
By my troth, I speak my thought.

CLAUDIO:
And, in faith, my lord, I spoke mine.

BENEDICK:
And by my two faiths and troths, my lord,
I spoke mine.

CLAUDIO:
That I love her, I feel.

DON PEDRO:
That she is worthy, I know.

BENEDICK:
That I neither feel she should be loved,
nor know she should be worthy, is the

*(enter UC Xing C, Cl rise)*

*(bows to DP on 'my allegiance')*

*(Xing to US end of bench)*

*(Xing to DL of DP)*

opinion that fire cannot melt out of me.
I will die with it at the stake.

DON PEDRO:
You were always a true-blue non-believer
when it came to worshipping beauty.

BENEDICK:
In that a woman conceived me, I thank
her. In that she brought me up, I likewise
give her thanks. But all women should pardon
me. Because I will not give them the wrong
of mistrust, I will give myself the right
to distrust; and the upshot is—I will remain
a bachelor.

DON PEDRO:
I shall see you, before I die, become weak-
kneed with love.

BENEDICK:
With anger, with sickness, or with hunger,
my lord, but not with love!

DON PEDRO:
Well, if you ever waver in your faith, you'll
be the butt of many a joke.

BENEDICK:
If I do, hang me and shoot at me.

DON PEDRO:
We'll see. In time, even the wildest bull
submits to the harness.

BENEDICK:
The wildest bull may be tamed, but if sensible
Benedick ever wear a harness, take the bull's
horns and set them on my head and hang a
sign around my neck that says, 'Here you
see Benedick—the married man.'

DON PEDRO:
Well, you'll come 'round in time. For
now, good Signior Benedick, go to Leonato's,
send him my compliments and tell him I will

opinion that fire cannot melt out of me.
I will die in it at the stake.

DON PEDRO:
Thou wast ever an obstinate heretic in
the despite of beauty.

BENEDICK:
That a woman conceived me, I thank her.
That she brought me up, I likewise give
her most humble thanks. But all women          *(Xing DLC)*
should pardon me. Because I will not do
them the wrong to mistrust any, I will
do myself the right to trust none; and
the fine is—I will live a bachelor.            *(turning back to them)*

DON PEDRO:
I shall see thee, ere I die, look pale          *(Xing to Ben)*
with love.

BENEDICK:
With anger, with sickness, or with hunger,
my lord, not with love!

DON PEDRO:
Well, if ever thou dost fall from this
faith, thou wilt prove a notable argument.

BENEDICK:
If I do, hang me and shoot at me!

DON PEDRO:
Well, as time shall try. 'In time the           *(Xing back to Cl)*
savage bull doth bear the yoke.'

BENEDICK:
The savage bull may; but if ever the            *(following DP)*
sensible Benedick bear it, pluck off the
bull's horns and set them in my forehead,
and in great letters signify, 'Here you may
see Benedick, the married man.'

DON PEDRO:
Well, you will temporize with the hours.
In the meantime, good Signior Benedick,
repair to Leonato's, commend me to him

come to his supper; for he has certainly
gone to an awful lot of trouble.


BENEDICK:
I have almost enough sense in me for
such an errand; and so I leave you. *[exit
Benedick]*

CLAUDIO:
My lord, your highness could do me a
favor.

DON PEDRO:
I am yours to command. Show me how and I
will do it.

CLAUDIO:
Does Leonato have any sons, my lord?

DON PEDRO:
No children but Hero, she's his only heir.
Are you in love with her, Claudio?

CLAUDIO:
Oh my lord, when you led us to these
wars just ended, I saw her with a soldier's
eye, liking her, but having a more important
task than to turn that liking into love.
But now that I've returned and thoughts
of war are gone, in their place sweet and
delicate desires have come rushing in telling
me how lovely Hero is!

DON PEDRO:
If you do love Hero, I will broach the subject
with her and with her father, and you will
have her.

CLAUDIO:
How generously you come to the aid of a lover
whom you recognize by his lovesick look!

DON PEDRO:
You're in love and I will help you find a
cure for it. I know we shall have partying

and tell him I will not fail him at
supper; for indeed he hath made great
preparation.

BENEDICK:
I have almost matter enough in me for
such an embassage; and so I leave you.
*[exit Benedick]*

*(bows exaggeratedly to DP,
exits UC)*

CLAUDIO:
My liege, your Highness now may do me
good.

DON PEDRO:
My love is thine to teach. Teach it and
see how apt it is to learn.

*(sits SL end of bench, gestures
for Cl to sit next to him)*

CLAUDIO:
Hath Leonato any son, my lord?

DON PEDRO:
No child but Hero, she's his only heir.
Dost thou affect her, Claudio?

CLAUDIO:
O my lord, when you went onward on this
ended action, I looked upon her with a
soldier's eye, that liked, but had a
rougher task in hand than to drive liking
to the name of love. But now I am returned,
and war-thoughts have left, in their places
come thronging soft and delicate desires,
all prompting me how fair Hero is!

DON PEDRO:
If thou dost love Hero, I will break with
her and with her father, and thou shalt
have her.

CLAUDIO:
How sweetly you do minister to love that
know love's grief by his complexion!

DON PEDRO:
Thou lovest and I will fit thee with the
remedy. I know we shall have revelling

*(rising, Cl follows suit, they
start Xing UC during speech)*

**Act One · Scene 1**   **vernacular**

tonight—I will disguise myself and pretend to be you and tell fair Hero that I am Claudio and I'll reveal my heart to her. Afterwards, I'll speak to her father and the result will be—she will be yours! Let's get to it immediately. *[they exit]*

**Act One · Scene 2**   **scene analysis**

Antonio tells his brother about the conversation between Don Pedro and Claudio that was overheard by one of Antonio's servants. The servant mistakenly reported that Don Pedro is in love with Hero and intends to profess his love that very night. Leonato decides to tell Hero the news.

**Act One · Scene 2**   **vernacular**

*[enter Leonato & Antonio]*
ANTONIO:
Brother, I can tell you some remarkable news that you never dreamt of.

LEONATO:
Is it good?

ANTONIO:
As time will tell. The Prince and Count Claudio, while walking in my orchard, were overheard by one of my servants. The Prince told Claudio that he loved my niece—your daughter—and meant to confess it tonight, and if he found her agreeable, he meant to immediately speak with you about it.

LEONATO:
Has the fellow any brains that told you this?

ANTONIO:
I will send for him and question him yourself.

LEONATO:
No, no, we'll let it remain as a dream till it shows itself to be real. But I will tell my daughter about it, so she may be better prepared with an answer, if it proves to be true. *[they exit]*

tonight—I will assume thy part in some disguise and tell fair hero I am Claudio, and I'll unclasp my heart. Then after, to her father will I break, and the conclusion is—she shall be thine! In practice let us put it presently. *[they exit]*

*(exit UC)*

*[enter Leonato & Antonio]*
ANTONIO:
Brother, I can tell you strange news that you dreamt not of.

*(enter DR Xing towards DL)*
*(talking while they walk, stopping as needed)*

LEONATO:
Are they good?

ANTONIO:
As the event stamps them. The Prince and Count Claudio, walking in mine orchard, were overheard by a man of mine. The Prince discovered to Claudio that he loved my niece—your daughter—and meant to acknowledge it this night, and if he found her accordant, he meant to instantly break with you of it.

LEONATO:
Hath the fellow any wit that told you this?

ANTONIO:
I will send for him and question him yourself.

LEONATO:
No, no, we will hold it as a dream till it appear itself. But I will acquaint my daughter withal, that she may be the better prepared for an answer, if peradventure this be true. *[they exit]*

*(exit DL)*

In Act 1 scene 3 we learn about Don John, the bastard brother of Don Pedro. Conrade, a friend and associate, is questioning him about the cause of his sadness. Don John tells him that he is basically a miserably unhappy person who has no cause to be happy and does not wish to change.

Borachio, another of Don John's men, comes to tell him that he has news of a possible marriage. Borachio says he overheard the Prince tell Claudio that he would woo Hero on Claudio's behalf. Don John expresses his dislike for Claudio, who he claims is receiving all the glory for his downfall, and asks his friends to assist him in thwarting Claudio. They agree to help him.

*[enter Don John & Conrade]*

CONRADE:
What the hell, my lord! Why are you so excessively sad?

DON JOHN:
There is no limit to the cause of my sadness, therefore my sadness is limitless.

CONRADE:
You should listen to reason.

DON JOHN:
And when I have heard it, what good will it bring?

CONRADE:
If not an immediate remedy, then at least it will teach you patience.

DON JOHN:
I cannot hide what I am—I must be sad when I have cause; eat when I'm hungry; sleep when I am drowsy; laugh when I am merry and suck up to no man's ego.

CONRADE:
Yes, but you musn't act this way till you can do it without risking censure. You have lately opposed your brother, and he only recently took you back into his favor, where it's not possible for you to remain if you don't make yourself agreeable. You must learn to act in your own best interests.

DON JOHN:
I'd rather be an ugly weed in a hedge than a rose in his favor, and it suits me better to be despised by all than to put on a front to steal anyone's approval. I am a straight-forward villain. If I could speak my mind I'd curse; if I were

| Act One · Scene 3 **original abridged** | Act One · Scene 3 **stage directions** |
|---|---|
| *[enter Don John & Conrade]*<br>CONRADE:<br>What the goodyear, my lord! Why are you thus out of measure sad? | *(enter DJ UL, X US of arbor, sit on bench, sulking, after a beat, Con enter UL, X L of arbor, put foot up on left end of bench, watch DJ for a beat, then speak)* |
| DON JOHN:<br>There is no measure in the occasion that breeds, therefore the sadness is without limit. | |
| CONRADE:<br>You should hear reason. | |
| DON JOHN:<br>And when I have heard it, what blessing brings it? | |
| CONRADE:<br>If not a present remedy, at least a patient sufferance. | |
| DON JOHN:<br>I cannot hide what I am—I must be sad when I have cause; eat when I have stomach; sleep when I am drowsy; laugh when I am merry and claw no man in his humor. | |
| CONRADE:<br>Yea, but you must not make the full show of this till you may do it without controlment. You have of late stood out against your brother, and he hath ta'en you newly into his grace, where it is impossible you should take true root but by the fair weather that you make your-self. It is needful that you frame the season for your own harvest. | *(sit L of DJ)* |
| DON JOHN:<br>I had rather be a canker in a hedge than a rose in his grace, and it better fits my blood to be disdained of all than to fashion a carriage to rob love from any. I am a plain-dealing villain. If I had my mouth I would bite; if I had my liberty I | *(X DR of C)* |

free to act, I'd do as I please. In the meantime, let me be as I am and don't try to alter me. *[enter Borachio]* What's the news, Borachio?

BORACHIO:
I came here from the banquet. The Prince your brother is royally entertained by Leonato, and I can give you news of an intended marriage.

DON JOHN:
Can we use it to make mischief? What fool sets himself up for such a bad time?

BORACHIO:
Indeed, it is your brother's right-hand man.

DON JOHN: *[sarcastically]*
Who? The wonderful Claudio?

BORACHIO:
Yes, he.

DON JOHN:
Who is it, who? Who's he got his eye on?

BORACHIO:
Indeed, on Hero, the daughter and heir of Leonato.

DON JOHN:
A ripe little chickadee! How did you discover this?

BORACHIO:
As I was airing out a musty room, the Prince and Claudio came in engaged in serious conversation. I hid myself behind the curtains and heard them agree that the Prince would woo Hero, and having obtained her hand, give her to Count Claudio.

DON JOHN:
This could prove fuel for my fire. That

Act One · Scene 3  **original abridged**

Act One · Scene 3    **stage directions**

would do my liking. In the meantime, let
me be that I am and seek not to alter me.
Who comes here? *[enter Borachio]* What
news, Borachio?

*(turn back to Con)*

*(Bor enter UC)*

BORACHIO:
I came yonder from a great supper. The
Prince your brother is royally entertained by Leonato, and I can give you
intelligence of an intended marriage.

*(Xing to DJ)*

DON JOHN:
Will it serve for any model to build
mischief on? What fool betroths himself
to unquietness?

BORACHIO:
Marry, it is your brother's right hand.

DON JOHN: *[sarcastically]*
Who? The most exquisite Claudio?

BORACHIO:
Even he.

*(Con X to L of Bor)*

DON JOHN:
And who, and who? Which way looks he?

*(all three start Xing DC)*

BORACHIO:
Marry, on Hero, the daughter and heir
of Leonato.

Don John:
A very forward March-chick! How came you
to this?

BORACHIO:
As I was smoking a musty room, comes the
Prince and Claudio in sad conference. I
whipped me behind the arras and there
heard it agreed that the Prince should
woo Hero, and having obtained her, give
her to Count Claudio.

*(by now they are DC)*

DON JOHN:
This may prove food to my displeasure.

young upstart has gained all the glory
I have lost. If I can trip him up in any
way, I'll count myself happy every day.
You will assist me?

CONRADE:
To the death, my lord.

DON JOHN:
Shall we go see what's to be done?

BORACHIO:
We're here to serve your lordship.
*[they exit]*

Act Two • Scene 1     **scene analysis**

It is after supper and Leonato, Antonio, Hero, and Beatrice are having a chat. The subject is Don John. Beatrice says that he always looks so sour that merely seeing him gives her indigestion. She then brings Benedick into the conversation, saying that the perfect man would be the one created halfway between Don John, who never says a word, and Benedick, who is forever jabbering. Leonato tells Beatrice that her sharp tongue will prevent her from ever getting a husband, and she tells him that she considers that a blessing.

Antonio turns the conversation back to the possibility of the Prince proposing to Hero, and Beatrice takes the opportunity to elaborate on her own thoughts about marriage.

As the masked guests enter, the family members don their disguises, and there is music and a dance. Don Pedro is partnered with Hero, and as they dance off, we realize that he will probably use the opportunity to propose to her. Borachio dances with Margaret and they flirt. Beatrice and Benedick dance. They pretend not to know who they are dancing with and take the opportunity to jibe one another. Benedick tells Beatrice that he has heard that she is disdainful and that her wit is hackneyed. Beatrice refers to Benedick as the Prince's dull-witted, slanderous jester.

The dancers depart, leaving Claudio, Don John,

Act Two • Scene 1      vernacular

*[enter Leonato, Antonio, Hero & Beatrice]*
LEONATO:
Wasn't Count John here at supper?

ANTONIO:
I didn't see him.

BEATRICE:
How very sour that gentleman looks! I never see him but I've got heart-burn for an hour.

HERO:
He has a very melancholy disposition.

BEATRICE:
The perfect man would be the one created just between him and Benedick. The one is just like a portrait and says nothing, and the other too like the spoilt brat of an indulgent mommy, always chattering.

LEONATO:
Truly, niece, you will never get a husband if you speak so shrewishly.

## Act One · Scene 3  original abridged

That young start-up hath all the glory
of my overthrow. If I can cross him any
way, I bless myself every way. You will
assist me?

CONRADE:
To the death, my lord.

DON JOHN:
Shall we go prove what's to be done?

BORACHIO:
We'll wait upon your lordship.
*[they exit]*

## Act One · Scene 3  stage directions

*(Xing L of arbor, exit UL as . . .)*

## Act Two · Scene 1  original abridged

*[enter Leonato, Antonio, Hero & Beatrice]*
LEONATO:
Was not Count John here at supper?

ANTONIO:
I saw him not.

BEATRICE:
How tartly that gentleman looks! I never
can see him but I am heart-burned an
hour after.

HERO:
He is of a very melancholy disposition.

BEATRICE:
He were an excellent man that were made
just in the mid-way between him and
Benedick. The one is too like an image
and says nothing, and the other too like
my lady's eldest son, evermore tattling.

LEONATO:
By my troth, niece, thou wilt never get
a husband if thou be so shrewd of thy
tongue.

## Act Two · Scene 1  stage directions

*(. . . Leo enters UC, followed
by Ant, they X to UL bench,
sit, Leo L of Ant, Bea & Her
enter UC, Bea Xing R of C,
Her X R of Ant, all have masks)*

## Act Two · Scene 1 — scene analysis

*Cont.*

and Borachio onstage. Don John and Borachio are aware that the masked figure is Claudio but approach him as "Benedick." Claudio responds to the name, and Don John and Borachio proceed to tell him that they know that the Prince is in love with Hero. They say that "Benedick" should dissuade him from her because she is unworthy of him.

Left alone, Claudio determines that no man can trust another when it comes to affairs of the heart. At this point, Benedick enters and informs Claudio that the Prince has courted Hero. Claudio goes off in a huff, and Benedick, still smarting from the wounds Beatrice inflicted on him during the dance, vows revenge.

Don Pedro, Hero, and Leonato come on in search of Claudio. Benedick reports that he has gone off to sulk after hearing the news that the Prince had wooed Hero. The Prince explains to Benedick that he was merely acting as Claudio's go-between in obtaining Hero's hand. He goes on to tell Benedick that Beatrice has a bone to pick with him. Don Pedro says that Beatrice told him that the man who danced with her told her that Benedick had insulted her. Benedick flies off into a rage about how Beatrice has "misused" him, and then goes on about what an awful harpy she is.

At this moment Beatrice arrives. Benedick makes a point of asking to be sent to the far ends of the earth so as to be able to avoid her. When the Prince tells him that he has no errand to send him on, Benedick exits with a parting shot to Beatrice calling her "Lady Tongue"!

After revealing something of her past history with Benedick, Beatrice reports that she has fulfilled her task of fetching Count Claudio.

The Prince observes that Claudio seems out of sorts, and Beatrice tells him that she believes Claudio is suffering from jealousy. The Prince tells Claudio that he has no cause to be jealous—that he has wooed Hero for his sake, discussed the proposition with Leonato, and that Hero is his. Leonato reinforces this, and the dumbfounded Claudio has to be prompted by Beatrice to speak to his love.

Beatrice then makes note of her own single state, and the Prince offers to get a husband for her. Beatrice jokingly says that she would rather have one begot by the Prince's father and asks if

## Act Two · Scene 1 — vernacular

BEATRICE:
For which blessing I thank God on my knees every morning and evening. Lord I could not stand a husband!

ANTONIO:
Well, niece, I trust you will be ruled by your father.

BEATRICE:
Yes, truly. It is my cousin's duty to make a curtsy and say, 'Father, if it pleases you.' But even so, cousin, let him be a handsome fellow, or else make another curtsy and say, 'Father, if it pleases me.'

LEONATO:
Well, niece, I hope one day to see you fitted with a husband.

BEATRICE:
No, uncle, I don't want one. Adam's sons are my brothers, and truly I think it's a sin to marry my relatives.

LEONATO:
Daughter, remember what I told you. If the Prince asks you that question, you know your answer.

BEATRICE:
The problem will be with the music, cousin, if you're not wooed in a timely manner. If the Prince push too fast, tell him there is a proper tempo to everything and therefore woo in time to the music. Because listen to me Hero, wooing, wedding, and repenting is as a Scotch jig, a waltz, and the can-can. The first stage is hot and hasty like a Scotch jig and just as outlandish; the wedding is proper, demure as the box step, full of solemnity and ritual; and then comes reality and with his fallen arches, he falls into the can-can till he falls on his can and can't any longer.

| Act Two·Scene 1 **original abridged** | Act Two·Scene 1 **stage directions** |
|---|---|

**BEATRICE:**
For the which blessing I am at Him upon my knees every morning and evening. Lord I could not endure a husband!

*(hands together in mock prayer)*

**ANTONIO:**
Well, niece, I trust you will be ruled by your father.

**BEATRICE:**
Yes, faith. It is my cousin's duty to make curtsy and say, 'Father, as it please you.' But yet for all that, cousin, let him be a handsome fellow, or else make another curtsy and say, 'Father, as it please me.'

*(Bea demonstrating curtsy)*

*(Xing R of Her)*

*(another curtsy)*

**LEONATO:**
Well, niece, I hope to see you one day fitted with a husband.

**BEATRICE:**
No, uncle, I'll none. Adam's sons are my brethren, and truly I hold it a sin to match in my kindred.

**LEONATO:**
Daughter, remember what I told you. If the Prince do solicit you in that kind, you know your answer.

**BEATRICE:**
The fault will be in the music, cousin, if you be not wooed in good time. If the Prince be too important, tell him there is measure in everything, and so dance out the answer. For hear me Hero, wooing, wedding, and repenting is as a Scotch jig, a measure, and a cinquepace. The first suit is hot and hasty, like a Scotch jig and full as fantastical; the wedding, mannerly modest, as a measure, full of state and ancientry; and then comes repentance and with his bad legs falls into the cinquepace faster and faster till he sink into his grave.

*(take Her's hand and guide her DR & seat her on US end of bench, Bea use C area to demonstrate dance steps for Her's benefit, however little or much actress desires to do this)*

*(all laugh and applaud Bea)*

*Cont.*
he has any brothers. The Prince offers himself.
Beatrice must find a graceful way out of the hole
she has just dug. She attempts this through flattery,
and the Prince lets her off the hook. Leonato then
sends her off on some errands.

The Prince determines that Beatrice and
Benedick would make a perfect couple. He pro-
poses that they use the time between now and the
wedding to gull (or trick) Beatrice and Benedick
into falling in love with each other. The others
agree to assist him.

**LEONATO:**
Cousin, you've got a quick wit.

**BEATRICE:**
I have a good eye, uncle—I can see the
obvious!

**LEONATO:**
The revelers are entering; make room.

*[enter Don Pedro, Claudio, Benedick, Don
John, Borachio & Margaret]*

**DON PEDRO:**
Lady, will you dance around with your
admirer?

**HERO:**
If you promise to tread lightly and look
sweetly and say nothing, I'll dance with
you—especially when I dance out of sight.

**DON PEDRO:**
With me accompanying you?

**HERO:**
I may say yes if I please.

**DON PEDRO:**
And when will it please you to say yes?

**HERO:**
When I like your looks.

**DON PEDRO:**
Speak soft when you speak of love.

**BORACHIO:**
Well, I wish you did like me.

**MARGARET:**
It's better I don't for your own sake,
for I have many bad qualities.

**BORACHIO:**
Name one.

## Act Two · Scene 1   original abridged

LEONATO:
Cousin, you apprehend passing shrewdly.

BEATRICE:
I have a good eye, uncle—I can see a church by daylight!

LEONATO:
The revelers are entering; make room.

[enter Don Pedro, Claudio, Benedick, Don John, Borachio & Margaret]

DON PEDRO:
Lady, will you walk about with your friend?

HERO:
So you walk softly and look sweetly and say nothing, I am yours for the walk—especially when I walk away.

DON PEDRO:
With me in your company?

HERO:
I may say so when I please.

DON PEDRO:
And when please you to say so?

HERO:
When I like your favor.

DON PEDRO:
Speak low if you speak love.

BORACHIO:
Well, I would you did like me.

MARGARET:
So would not I for your own sake, for I have many ill qualities.

BORACHIO:
Which is one?

## Act Two · Scene 1   stage directions

(music* plays, all wear masks in this scene, Mar & Bor enter DR, move bench to DR side of stage, as Her & Bea run behind arbor to don masks, as DP enters UC, Xing C, Mar & Bor X US of DP, as Cl enters UC & X to L of Leo, as Her enters DS of arbor Xing to DL of Cl, Ben enter UC, Bea X to Ben, they stand US of Mar & Bor, as DJ enters UC, X to stand UR, this is all done quickly) (extends arm to Her, Her X & take his hand, they dance* moving DC)

(dancing to DRC)

(end RC, stop, watch others dance)

(Bor & Mar dance to DC)

MARGARET:
I say my prayers out loud.

BORACHIO:
I love you even more—I can
cry 'Amen.'

BEATRICE:
Won't you tell me who told you so?

BENEDICK: *[trying to disguise his voice]*
No, pardon me.

BEATRICE:
And you won't tell me who you are?

BENEDICK:
Not now.

BEATRICE:
That I was disdainful, and that my wit
came from 'The Sophomore Joke Book'—
well, this was Signior Benedick that said this.

BENEDICK:
Who is he?

BEATRICE:
I am sure you are well aware of him.

BENEDICK:
I'm not, believe me.

BEATRICE:
Has he never made you laugh?

BENEDICK:
Come on, who is he?

BEATRICE:
Why, he is the Prince's jester, a very dull
fool. His only talent is in inventing
ridiculous slanders. None but the frivolous
find delight in him, and their fascination
is not with his wittiness but with his
wickedness. I am sure he is in this bunch;
I wish he'd have picked me.

| Act Two·Scene 1 **original abridged** | Act Two·Scene 1 **stage directions** |
| --- | --- |

**MARGARET:**
I say my prayers aloud.

*(continue dance to DR bench)*

**BORACHIO:**
I love you the better—the hearers may cry 'Amen.'

*(they sit on bench & watch)*

**BEATRICE:**
Will you not tell me who told you so?

*(Bea and Ben dance to DC)*

**BENEDICK:** *[trying to disguise his voice]*
No, you shall pardon me.

**BEATRICE:**
Nor will you not tell me who you are?

*(as Ben & Bea talk, all except DJ listen & laugh appropriately as they jibe each other)*

**BENEDICK:**
Not now.

**BEATRICE:**
That I was disdainful, and that I had my good wit out of the 'Hundred Merry Tales'—well, this was Signior Benedick that said so.

**BENEDICK:**
What's he?

**BEATRICE:**
I am sure you know him well enough.

**BENEDICK:**
Not I, believe me.

**BEATRICE:**
Did he never make you laugh?

**BENEDICK:**
I pray you what is he?

**BEATRICE:**
Why, he is the Prince's jester, a very dull fool. Only his gift is in devising impossible slanders. None but libertines delight in him, and the commendation is not in his wit but in his villainy. I am sure he is in the fleet I would he had boarded me.

**Act Two · Scene 1          vernacular**

BENEDICK:
When I meet the gentleman, I'll tell him what you said.

BEATRICE:
Oh do, do. He'll just crack a joke or two about me, which, perhaps not noted or not laughed at, throws him into a depression. We must follow the leaders.

BENEDICK:
In every good thing.

*[all exit except Don John, Borachio & Claudio]*
DON JOHN:
Only one mask remains.

BORACHIO:
And that is Claudio. I know him by his walk.

DON JOHN: *[to Claudio]*
Aren't you Signior Benedick?

CLAUDIO: *[trying to sound like Benedick]*
You know me well, I am he.

DON JOHN:
Signior, you are very close to my brother. He is in love with Hero. I beg you to talk him out of her; she is not good enough for him.

CLAUDIO:
How do you know he loves her?

DON JOHN:
I heard him vow his love.

BORACHIO:
So did I, and he swore he would marry her.

DON JOHN:
Come, let's go to the banquet. *[Don John & Borachio exit]*

| Act Two·Scene 1 **original abridged** | Act Two·Scene 1 **stage directions** |
|---|---|

BENEDICK:
When I know the gentleman, I'll tell him
what you say.

BEATRICE:
Do, do. He'll but break a comparison or
two on me, which peradventure not marked
or not laughed at, strikes him into
melancholy. We must follow the leaders.

BENEDICK:
In every good thing.

*[all exit except Don John, Borachio &
Claudio]*
DON JOHN:
But one visor remains.

*(music ends on 'melancholy,'
all applaud, DP & Her start
Xing UC, Ant & Leo follow,
Cl sit DS end of bench, as
Bea & Ben follow UC, as Mar
& Bor replace bench & start
UC, as DJ intercepts Bor, Mar
curtsy to DJ & exit)*

BORACHIO:
And that is Claudio. I know him by his
bearing.

DON JOHN: *[to Claudio]*
Are not you Signior Benedick?

*(X DS to Cl)*

CLAUDIO: *[trying to sound like Benedick]*
You know me well, I am he.

DON JOHN:
Signior, you are very near my brother. He
is enamored on Hero. I pray you dissuade
him from her; she is no equal for his
birth.

CLAUDIO:
How know you he loves her?

DON JOHN:
I heard him swear his affection.

BORACHIO:
So did I too, and he swore he would
marry her.

DON JOHN:
Come, let us to the banquet. *[Don John &
Borachio exit]*

*(DJ & Bor exit UC)*

CLAUDIO:
So I answer to the name of Benedick, but hear this horrible news with Claudio's ears. It's certain; the Prince woos for himself! Friends are reliable in everything except in the affairs of love. Therefore those in love should speak for themselves; let every lovesick heart deal on its own, and trust no substitute. Farewell therefore, Hero!

*[enter Benedick]*
BENEDICK:
Count Claudio?

CLAUDIO:
Yes, it's me.

BENEDICK:
The Prince has gotten your Hero.

CLAUDIO:
I wish him joy with her.

BENEDICK:
Did you ever think the Prince would have treated you this way?

CLAUDIO:
Leave me alone.

BENEDICK:
Oh!—striking out like a blind man! Don't confuse the message with the messenger!

CLAUDIO:
If you won't leave me, I'll leave you.
*[Claudio exits]*

BENEDICK: *[looking off after Claudio]*
Alas, poor little fool! But, that the Lady Beatrice should know me and not know me! The Prince's fool! Ha! I don't have that reputation. It is the mean and bitter disposition of Beatrice that interprets the world with

CLAUDIO:
Thus answer I in name of Benedick, but
hear these ill news with the ears of
Claudio. 'Tis certain; the Prince woos
for himself! Friendship is constant in
other things save in the affairs of love.
Therefore all hearts in love use their
own tongues; let every eye negotiate for
itself, and trust no agent. Farewell
therefore, Hero!

*[enter Benedick]*                                    *(enter UC, X to Cl & sit)*
BENEDICK:
Count Claudio?

CLAUDIO:
Yea, the same.

BENEDICK:
The Prince hath got your Hero.

CLAUDIO:
I wish him joy of her.

BENEDICK:
Did you ever think the Prince would have
served you thus?

CLAUDIO:
I pray you leave me.

BENEDICK:
Ho!—now you strike like the blind man!
'Twas the boy that stole your meat, and
you'll beat the post.

CLAUDIO:
If it will not be, I'll leave you.
*[Claudio exits]*                                     *(exits SL)*

BENEDICK: *[looking off after Claudio]*
Alas, poor hurt fowl! But, that my Lady        *(rise, Xing DRC during speech)*
Beatrice should know me and not know me!
The Prince's fool! Ha! I am not so reputed.
It is the base, though bitter, disposition
of Beatrice that puts the world into her

her own perspectives and so brands me.
Well, I'll be revenged however I can.

*[enter Don Pedro, Hero & Leonato]*
DON PEDRO:
Now, Signior, where's the Count?

BENEDICK:
Truly, my lord, I found him here melancholy. I told him—and I think I told
the truth—that your Grace had gotten
the consent of this young lady, and I
offered to accompany him to a willow tree
for a whipping.

DON PEDRO:
A whipping? For what fault?

BENEDICK:
That basic sin of the schoolboy who being
overjoyed at finding a bird's nest, shows
it to his companion, who steals it.

DON PEDRO:
The one who steals is the sinner.

BENEDICK:
You! Who, as I understand, have stolen his
bird's nest.

DON PEDRO:
I will only teach the little birds to sing
and then return them to their owner.

BENEDICK:
If they end up singing a lovesong, then truly,
you speak honestly.

DON PEDRO:
The Lady Beatrice has a bone to pick with
you. The gentleman that danced with her told
her you have done her a grave injustice.

BENEDICK:
Oh, she abused me beyond what a brick
could endure! An oak tree with only

person and so gives me out. Well, I'll be
revenged as I may.

*[enter Don Pedro, Hero & Leonato]*
DON PEDRO:
Now, Signior, where's the Count?

BENEDICK:
Troth, my lord, I found him here
melancholy. I told him—and I think I
told him true—that your Grace had got
the good will of this young lady, and I
offered him my company to a willow tree
to be whipped.

DON PEDRO:
To be whipped? What's his fault?

BENEDICK:
The flat transgression of a schoolboy who,
being overjoyed at finding a bird's nest,
shows it his companion, and he steals it.

DON PEDRO:
The transgression is in the stealer.

BENEDICK:
You! Who, as I take it, have stolen his
bird's nest.

DON PEDRO:
I will but teach them to sing and restore
them to the owner.

BENEDICK:
If their singing answer your saying,
by my faith, you say honestly.

DON PEDRO:
The Lady Beatrice hath a quarrel to you.
The gentleman that danced with her told
her she is much wronged by you.

BENEDICK:
O, she misused me past the endurance
of a block! An oak with but one green

*(end sitting on DS end of DR bench)*

*(enter UC X C, DP R of Her,
Her R of Leo)*

*(Xing to Ben)*

*(sitting next to Ben)*

*(rise, X DLC)*

one green leaf left on it would have
mustered the strength to answer her.
She told me not realizing it was me—
that I was the Prince's jester, that I
was as dull as an ice cube thawing.
She lobbed insult upon insult with such
unbelievable speed that I stood there
like a man at a bull's-eye with a whole
army shooting at me. She speaks daggers,
and every word stabs. If her breath were as
terrible as her wisecracks, nobody could
live near her. I wouldn't marry her, even if
she possessed everything Adam had before
he was thrown out of the garden. Surely—
uneasiness, horror, and great disturbances
follow her everywhere!

DON PEDRO:
Look, here she comes.

*[Beatrice & Claudio enter]*
BENEDICK:
Will your Grace command me to any employment at the edge of the universe? I will
run the most insignificant errand to the
opposite side of the world that you can
devise to send me on; I will fetch a tooth-
pick from the furthest part of Asia. Do
anything, rather than exchange three words'
talk with this harpy. You have nothing for
me to do?

DON PEDRO:
Nothing, but to share your company.

BENEDICK:
Oh, God, sir, here's a dish I don't like!
I cannot endure my Lady Tongue.
*[exit Benedick]*

DON PEDRO:
Oh, my lady—you have lost Signior
Benedick's heart.

BEATRICE:
Yes, my lord, he lent it to me for a while,

leaf on it would have answered her. She
told me—not thinking I had been myself—
that I was the Prince's jester, that I
was duller than a great thaw, huddling
jest upon jest with such impossible
conveyance that I stood like a man at
a mark, with a whole army shooting at me.
She speaks poniards, and every word stabs.
If her breath were as terrible as her
terminations, there were no living near
her! Come, talk not of her. I would not
marry her, though she were endowed with
all that Adam had left him before he
transgressed. Indeed—disquiet, horror,
and perturbation follows her!

DON PEDRO:
Look, here she comes.

[Beatrice & Claudio enter]
BENEDICK:
Will your Grace command me any service
to the world's end? I will go on the
slightest errand now to the Antipodes
that you can devise to send me on; I will
fetch a toothpicker from the furthest
inch of Asia. Do you any embassage,
rather than hold three words' conference
with this harpy. You have no employment
for me?

DON PEDRO:
None, but to desire your good company.

BENEDICK:
O God, sir, here's a dish I love not! I
cannot endure my Lady Tongue.
[exit Benedick]

DON PEDRO:
Come, lady, come—you have lost the
heart of Signior Benedick.

BEATRICE:
Indeed, my lord, he lent it me awhile,

(others enjoy and laugh at
Ben's humor, this spurs him
on, he loves an audience)

(after 'talk not of her' Ben
exits DL & immediately returns
and goes on talking)

(looking off SL)

(enter SL, stand & watch)

(X to DP & kneel)

(Her, Leo & DP laugh, Bea gloats)
(exits DR, as Bea X LC, Cl
lags behind)

(DP Xing to Bea, end DR of Her)

(taking a step DS to DP)

and I paid dearly for it—giving him twice
as much heart as he gave to me. Truly, once
before he won it playing falsely, therefore
your grace may well say that I have lost
it.

DON PEDRO:
You have put him down, lady, you have put
him down.

BEATRICE:
Which I hope he never does to me, my lord,
or I might become the mother of fools. I've
brought Count Claudio, whom you sent me
to seek.

DON PEDRO:
Why, what's wrong, Claudio? Why are you
sad?

CLAUDIO:
Not sad, my lord.

DON PEDRO:
How then—sick?

CLAUDIO:
Neither, my lord.

BEATRICE:
The Count is neither sad, nor sick, nor
merry, nor well; but he does look somewhat
jealous.

DON PEDRO:
Indeed, lady, I think your interpretation is true, though I swear, if he is,
his belief is false. Here, Claudio, I
wooed in your name, and Hero is yours.
I spoke with her father and he approves.
Name the wedding day, and God give you
joy!

LEONATO:
Count, take my daughter and along with her
a great dowry. His Grace has arranged the
marriage and all good graces bless it!

Act Two·Scene 1  **original abridged**

Act Two·Scene 1  **stage directions**

and I gave him use for it—a double
heart for his single one. Marry, once
before he won it with false dice, therefore your grace may well say I have lost
it.

DON PEDRO:
You have put him down, lady, you have put
him down.

BEATRICE:
So I would not he should do me, my lord,
lest I should prove the mother of fools.
I have brought Count Claudio, whom you
sent me to seek.

*(gesturing to Cl)*

DON PEDRO:
Why, how now, Count? Wherefore are you
sad?

CLAUDIO:
Not sad, my lord.

*(steps DL, facing DS)*

DON PEDRO:
How then—sick?

CLAUDIO:
Neither, my lord.

BEATRICE:
The Count is neither sad, nor sick, nor
merry, nor well; but something of that
jealous complexion.

DON PEDRO:
I' faith, lady, I think your blazon to
be true, though I'll be sworn, if he be
so, his conceit is false. Here, Claudio,
I have wooed in thy name, and fair Hero
is won. I have broke with her father and
his good will obtained. Name the day of
marriage, and God give thee joy!

*(Cl turns back to DP)*

LEONATO:
Count, take of me my daughter and with
her my fortunes. His Grace hath made the
match and all grace say amen to it!

*(brings Her to Cl & puts her
hand in his, Leo stands US
of them & watches, all repeat
'amen' after Leo's line)*

**Act Two · Scene 1**          **vernacular**

BEATRICE:
Speak Count, it's your cue.

CLAUDIO:
I am dumbstruck with joy. Lady, just as you are now mine, I am yours.

BEATRICE:
Speak, cousin, or—if you cannot—shut him up with a kiss and don't let him speak either.

DON PEDRO:
Indeed, lady, you have a cheerful spirit.

BEATRICE:
Yes, my lord, I thank it, poor dear, it keeps me out of the way of sorrow. My cousin tells him in his ear that he is in her heart.

CLAUDIO:
So she does, cousin.

BEATRICE:
Good Lord, send me a husband! Everyone in the world is paired but me.

DON PEDRO:
Lady Beatrice, I will get you one.

BEATRICE:
I would rather have one that your father begot. Does your Grace have a brother like you?

DON PEDRO:
Will you have me, lady?

BEATRICE:
No, my lord, unless I might have another for workdays; your Grace is too costly for everyday. But I beg your Grace to pardon me, I was born to speak only silliness and no sense.

| Act Two·Scene 1 **original abridged** | Act Two·Scene 1 **stage directions** |
|---|---|
| **BEATRICE:**<br>Speak Count, 'tis your cue. | *(after a beat, X R of Her, looking across to Cl)* |
| **CLAUDIO:**<br>Silence is the perfectest herald of joy. Lady, as you are mine, I am yours. | |
| **BEATRICE:**<br>Speak, cousin, or—if you cannot—stop his mouth with a kiss and let not him speak neither. | *(giving Her a gentle nudge)* |
| **DON PEDRO:**<br>In faith, lady, you have a merry heart. | *(Xing 2 steps to DC)* |
| **BEATRICE:**<br>Yea, my lord, I thank it, poor fool, it keeps on the windy side of care. My cousin tells him in his ear that he is in her heart. | *(Bea meets DP DC, Cl takes Her DLC & they whisper to each other)* |
| **CLAUDIO:**<br>And so she doth, cousin. | |
| **BEATRICE:**<br>Good Lord, for alliance! Thus goes everyone to the world but I. | |
| **DON PEDRO:**<br>Lady Beatrice, I will get you one. | |
| **BEATRICE:**<br>I would rather have one of your father's getting. Hath your Grace a brother like you? | |
| **DON PEDRO:**<br>Will you have me, lady? | |
| **BEATRICE:**<br>No, my lord, unless I might have another for working days; your Grace is too costly to wear everyday. But I beseech your Grace pardon me, I was born to speak all mirth and no matter. | |

**Act Two · Scene 1**          **vernacular**

DON PEDRO:
Your silence troubles me most, and being merry suits you best.

BEATRICE:
Cousins, God give you joy!

LEONATO:
Niece, will you tend to those things I told you about?

BEATRICE:
I beg your pardon, uncle. With your Grace's permission. *[Beatrice exits]*

DON PEDRO:
Truly, a good-natured lady.

LEONATO:
There are no depressing spirits in her my lord.

DON PEDRO:
She cannot stand to hear tell of a husband.

LEONATO:
Oh, by no means—she makes such fun of her wooers that they give up.

DON PEDRO:
She'd be an excellent wife for Benedick.

LEONATO:
Oh Lord, my lord, if they were married just a week, they'd drive each other crazy.

DON PEDRO:
Count Claudio, when do you plan to be married?

CLAUDIO:
Tomorrow, my lord!

LEONATO:
Not till Monday, my dear son, which

| Act Two · Scene 1 **original abridged** | Act Two · Scene 1    **stage directions** |
|---|---|

DON PEDRO:
Your silence most offends me, and to be
merry best becomes you.

BEATRICE:
Cousins, God give you joy!

*(Xing to Her)*

LEONATO:
Niece, will you look to those things I
told you of?

*(Xing to R of Bea)*

BEATRICE:
I cry you mercy, uncle. By your Grace's
pardon. *[Beatrice exits]*

*(curtsy to DP & exit UC)*

DON PEDRO:
By my troth, a pleasant-spirited lady.

*(Xing DR of Leo)*

LEONATO:
There's little of the melancholy element
in her my lord.

DON PEDRO:
She cannot endure to hear tell of a
husband.

LEONATO:
O, by no means—she mocks all her wooers
out of suit.

DON PEDRO:
She were an excellent wife for Benedick.

LEONATO:
O Lord, my lord, if they were but a week
married, they would talk themselves mad.

*(Her & Cl listen up to this)*

DON PEDRO:
Count Claudio, when mean you to go to
church?

CLAUDIO:
Tomorrow, my lord!

LEONATO:
Not till Monday, my dear son, which is

is a week away, and too short a time,
too, to get everything ready.

DON PEDRO: *[to Claudio]*
Oh come on, you shake your head at so
long a time, but I promise you, Claudio,
the time will not go boringly by. I will,
in the meantime, undertake a Herculean
labor, which is—to bring Signior Benedick
and the Lady Beatrice into a state of
monumental affection for one another. I've
no doubt we can accomplish this if you three
will assist me as I shall instruct you.

LEONATO:
My lord, I'm at your service, even if
it costs me ten sleepless nights.

CLAUDIO:
And I, my lord.

DON PEDRO:
And you too, gentle Hero?

HERO:
I will do anything within the bounds of
decency, my lord, to assist my cousin in
getting a good husband.

DON PEDRO:
And Benedick is not the least promising
husband that I know. He has a generous
disposition, is proven brave and without
a doubt he's honest. I will instruct you
how to deal with your cousin so that she
shall fall in love with Benedick; and I
*[to Leonato & Claudio]* with your help,
will work on Benedick, so that in spite
of his queasy stomach, he shall fall in
love with Beatrice. If we can do this,
Cupid's lost his bow and arrow—his glory
shall be ours—we are the true love-gods.
Go with me and I will fill you in. *[they
exit]*

hence just a sevennight, and a time to brief, too, to have all things answer my mind.

DON PEDRO: *[to Claudio]*
Come, you shake the head at so long a breathing, but I warrant thee, Claudio, the time shall not go dully by us. I will, in the interim, undertake one of Hercules labors, which is—to bring Signior Benedick and the Lady Beatrice into a mountain of affection the one with the other. I doubt not but to fashion it if you three will but minister such assistance as I shall give you direction.

LEONATO:
My lord, I am for you, though it cost me ten nights' watchings.

CLAUDIO:
And I, my lord.

DON PEDRO:
And you too, gentle Hero?

HERO:
I will do any modest office, my lord, to help my cousin to a good husband.

DON PEDRO:
And Benedick is not the unhopefulest husband that I know. He is of a noble strain, of approved valor, and confirmed honesty. I will teach you how to humor your cousin that she shall fall in love with Benedick; and I *[to Leonato & Claudio]* with your two helps, will so practice on Benedick, that in spite of his queasy stomach, he shall fall in love with Beatrice. If we can do this, Cupid is no longer an archer—his glory shall be ours—we are the only love-gods. Go with me and I will tell you my drift. *[they exit]*

*(Xing DS & around Leo to end up between Leo and Her, Leo counters R)*

*(puts arm around Leo's shoulder, they start UC, Cl & Her follow, exit UC)*

| Act Two • Scene 2 | **scene analysis** |
| --- | --- |

In this scene we see Borachio and Don John contriving their malicious plot to cross Claudio. Borachio tells Don John that he is "in the favor of Margaret" and that she will do whatever he asks of her. He says that he will get Margaret to pretend to be Hero and speak to him from Hero's bedroom window. He himself will then flirt with her, calling her "Hero." Don John's part will be to tell the Prince and Claudio that Hero is having an affair with Borachio and to convince them to come and witness this event the night before the intended marriage.

| Act Two • Scene 2 | **vernacular** |
| --- | --- |

*[enter Don John & Borachio]*
DON JOHN:
It's true, Count Claudio shall marry the daughter of Leonato.

BORACHIO:
Yes, my lord, but I can cross it up.

DON JOHN:
Any hindrance, any cross, any impediment will be medicinable to me. I am sick with displeasure of him. How can you cross up this marriage?

BORACHIO:
Not honestly, my lord, but so underhandedly that my dishonesty will not be seen.

DON JOHN:
Show me briefly how.

BORACHIO:
I think I told your lordship that Margaret, Hero's waiting gentlewoman, is very fond of me.

DON JOHN:
I remember.

BORACHIO:
I can, at any time of night, instruct her to look out of her lady's chamber window.

DON JOHN:
What good is that, that can prove evil to this marriage?

BORACHIO:
You have the power to mix up the poison. Go to the Prince your brother; tell him that he has damaged his honor by arranging this marriage for Claudio—whom you esteem so highly—to a tainted whore, like Hero.

DON JOHN:
What proof can I give them of that?

| Act Two·Scene 2 **original abridged** | Act Two·Scene 2 **stage directions** |
|---|---|

*[enter Don John & Borachio]*
DON JOHN:
It is so, Count Claudio shall marry the daughter of Leonato.

*(DJ enters UC, quickly Xing DLC, Bor follows him on & sits on UL bench)*

BORACHIO:
Yea, my lord, but I can cross it.

DON JOHN:
Any bar, any cross, any impediment will be medicinable to me. I am sick in displeasure to him. How canst thou cross this marriage?

*(Xing to SL end of UL bench)*

BORACHIO:
Not honestly, my lord, but so covertly that no dishonesty shall appear in me.

DON JOHN:
Show me briefly how.

BORACHIO:
I think I told your lordship how much I am in the favor of Margaret, the waiting gentlewoman to Hero.

DON JOHN:
I remember.

BORACHIO:
I can, at any instant of the night, appoint her to look out her lady's chamber window.

DON JOHN:
What life is in that, to be the death of this marriage?

*(X to DR bench, sit)*

BORACHIO:
The poison lies in you to temper. Go to the Prince your brother; tell him that he hath wronged his honor in marrying the renowned Claudio—whose estimation you mightily hold up—to a contaminated stale, such as Hero.

*(Xing to US of bench to stand behind DJ, DJ looking out front)*

DON JOHN:
What proof shall I make of that?

BORACHIO:
Proof enough to deceive the Prince, to torment Claudio, to destroy Hero, and to kill Leonato. Are you looking for anything else.

DON JOHN:
To spite them I will undertake anything.

BORACHIO:
Then go, find Don Pedro and Count Claudio. Tell them that you know that Hero loves me; convince the Prince and Claudio that you are in earnest—as if it is to protect your brother's honor and his friend's reputation that you have revealed this. They'll hardly believe it. So offer to give them proof—to see me at her bedroom window, hear me call Margaret 'Hero.' Bring them to see this the very night before the intended wedding. I will arrange things so that Hero shall be away— and it shall appear that Hero is, in fact, unfaithful.

DON JOHN:
I will set this in motion. Be clever with your part and you'll earn a thousand gold coins. *[they exit]*

This scene opens with a soliloquy by Benedick bemoaning the fact that his good friend Claudio has succumbed to the downfall of man—falling in love! He examines his own risks of becoming victim of this horrible fate and reassures himself that he will remain invincible until all the perfect qualities of womanhood be incorporated into one woman!

Benedick then sees the Prince, Leonato, and Claudio coming and decides to hide. They, spotting where he has hidden himself, proceed with their gulling plot to trick him into falling in love with Beatrice.

They talk of Beatrice's "love" for Benedick—the

*[enter Benedick]*
BENEDICK:
I wonder that one man, seeing how great a fool another man is when he commits himself to love, will—after having laughed at such foolishness in others—become the object of his own derision by falling in love; and such a man is Claudio. Could I be likewise converted? I can't be sure; I don't think so. Love may transform me, but I'll take an oath on it, till love has, he shall never make me such a fool. One woman is pretty,

**Act Two·Scene 2 original abridged**

BORACHIO:
Proof enough to misuse the Prince, to
vex Claudio, to undo Hero, and kill
Leonato. Look you for any other issue?

DON JOHN:
To spite them I will endeavor anything.

BORACHIO:
Go then, find Don Pedro and the Count
Claudio. Tell them that you know that
Hero loves me; intend a kind of zeal
both to the Prince and Claudio—as in
love of your brother's honor and his
friend's reputation you have discovered
thus. They will scarcely believe this.
Offer them instances—to see me at her
chamber window, hear me call Margaret
'Hero.' Bring them to see this the very
night before the intended wedding. I
will fashion the matter that Hero shall
be absent—and there shall appear seeming
truth of Hero's disloyalty.

DON JOHN:
I will put it in practice. Be cunning in
working this and thy fee is a thousand
ducats. *[they exit]*

**Act Two·Scene 2    stage directions**

*(X & sit L of DJ on bench)*

*(X DC, Bor follow to L of DJ)*

*(exit DL)*

**Act Two·Scene 3 original abridged**

*[enter Benedick]*
BENEDICK:
I do wonder that one man, seeing how much
another man is a fool when he dedicates
his behaviors to love, will—after he
hath laughed at such follies in others—
become the argument of his own scorn by
falling in love; and such a man is
Claudio. May I be so converted? I cannot
tell; I think not. Love may transform me,
but I'll take my oath on it, till he have,
he shall never make me such a fool. One

**Act Two·Scene 3    stage directions**

*(enter SR with glass of wine
& book, sit UL bench, place
wine on bench, open book, read
for a beat* or two, close book,
look out front & deliver
monologue* to audience, sipping
wine as desired)*

## Act Two · Scene 3          scene analysis

*Cont.*

news of which they supposedly got from Hero. When they realize they have gotten Benedick's attention, they go on to reel him in with examples of Beatrice's lovesickness and the torment in which she supposedly exists trying to hide her love from Benedick. Once he is hooked, they note that Hero and Margaret will have to spread "the same net" for Beatrice. They then decide to send Beatrice to fetch Benedick in to dinner.

Having been left alone, we see that Benedick has been totally taken in. He believes that Beatrice is in love with him and declares that her love "must be requited"! He praises himself for being man enough to hear talk of his faults and to be willing to correct them.

He realizes that he may have to suffer a certain amount of ridicule for reversing his long-held stance against marriage, but points out that with age a man's tastes alter and that he will not allow jibes and sarcasm to deter him from his course of action. "No," he says, "the world must be peopled!"

At this moment Beatrice appears to fulfill her assignment to call him in to dinner. Beatrice curtly carries out her mission, and Benedick interprets her curtness as obvious signs of love for him. He is a goner!

## Act Two · Scene 3          vernacular

yet I am well; another is wise, yet I am well; another is virtuous, yet I am well; but till all graces are found in one woman, one woman shall not be in my grace. Rich she shall be, that's certain; wise, or I'll none of her; virtuous, or I'll never cheapen her; fair, or I'll never look at her; mild, or don't come near me; a good conversationalist, an excellent musician, and her hair shall be—whatever color God pleases. Aha, the Prince and Monsieur Lovesick! I will hide.

*[enter Don Pedro, Leonato & Claudio]*
CLAUDIO:
How still the evening is, as if hushed on purpose.

DON PEDRO: *[aside]*
Do you see where Benedick has hidden himself?

CLAUDIO: *[aside]*
Oh, very well, my lord.

DON PEDRO:
Come here, Leonato, what was that you told me today, that your niece Beatrice was in love with Signior Benedick?

CLAUDIO:
Oh, yes! *[aside to Don Pedro]* Keep stalking, keep stalking, our pidgeon is perched. *[aloud]* I never thought that lady would love any man.

LEONATO:
No, neither did I, but it's so wonderful that she should dote so on Signior Benedick, whom she has always outwardly seemed to abhor.

BENEDICK: *[aside]*
Is it possible? Is that the way the wind blows?

woman is fair, yet I am well; another is
wise, yet I am well; another virtuous,
yet I am well; but till all graces be in
one woman, one woman shall not come in
my grace. Rich she shall be, that's certain;
wise, or I'll none; virtuous, or I'll
never cheapen her; fair, or I'll never
look on her; mild, or come not near me;
of good discourse, an excellent musician,
and her hair shall be—of what color it
please God. Ha, the Prince and Monsieur
Love! I will hide me.

[enter Don Pedro, Leonato & Claudio]
CLAUDIO:
How still the evening is, as hushed on
purpose.

DON PEDRO: [aside]
See where Benedick hath hid himself?

CLAUDIO: [aside]
O, very well, my lord.

DON PEDRO:
Come hither, Leonato, what was it you told
me today, that your niece Beatrice was in
love with Signior Benedick?

CLAUDIO:
O, ay! [aside to Don Pedro] Stalk on,
stalk on, the fowl sits. [aloud] I did
never think that lady would have loved
any man.

LEONATO:
No, nor I neither, but most wonderful
that she should so dote on Signior
Benedick, whom she hath in all outward
behaviors seemed ever to abhor.

BENEDICK: [aside]
Is't possible? Sits the wind in that
corner?

*(after 'please God' offstage
ad libs\* from UC, Ben X DS
& around L of arbor, take book
& glass, peek out from L side of arbor)*

*(enter DP, Leo & Cl UC, Xing
C, Leo C, DP L of Leo)*

*(DP indicating arbor, whispering\*
his aside\*)*

*(DP brings Leo to DR bench,
sit, as Cl tiptoes UR side
of arbor, peaks behind)*
*(Ben reacts to DP's line from L of
arbor, spraying mouthful of wine)*

*(X to C for 'O, ay', X to
behind Leo & DP for aside,
remain above bench)*

*(peaking out from L side of
arbor, note: Ben should leave
his props under the ladder)*

LEONATO:
Truly, my lord, I don't know what to
think of it—she loves him with such
raging emotions that it is almost
unimaginable.

DON PEDRO:
Maybe she's only feigning.

CLAUDIO:
Yes, perhaps.

LEONATO:
Oh God! Feigning? There was never
feigning of passion so like the truth
of passion.

DON PEDRO:
Why, what signs of passion does she exhibit?

CLAUDIO: *[aside]*
Bait the hook well, this fish will bite.

LEONATO:
What signs, my lord? She will sit . . .
you heard my daughter tell you how.

DON PEDRO:
How, how, I implore you? You amaze
me! I'd have thought her spirit had
been invincible against all assaults
of affection.

LEONATO:
I would have sworn it had, my lord,
especially against Benedick.

BENEDICK: *[aside]*
I'd think this was a trap, except that
the old fellow says it.

CLAUDIO: *[aside]*
He's hooked—keep it up.

DON PEDRO:
Has she let Benedick know of her
affection?

## Act Two·Scene 3 **original abridged**

## Act Two·Scene 3 **stage directions**

LEONATO:
By my troth my lord, I cannot tell what
to think of it—she loves him with an
enraged affection, it is past the
infinite of thought.

DON PEDRO:
Maybe she doth but counterfeit.

CLAUDIO:
Faith, like enough.

LEONATO:
O God! Counterfeit? There was never
counterfeit of passion came so near
the life of passion.

DON PEDRO:
Why, what effects of passion shows she?

CLAUDIO: *[aside]*
Bait the hook well, this fish will bite.

*(after line, X to UL bench, sit, to keep an 'ear' on Ben)*

LEONATO:
What effects, my lord? She will sit you . . .
you heard my daughter tell you how.

*(obviously forgets lines DP wrote for him, looks to DP & Cl for help)*

DON PEDRO:
How, how, I pray you? You amaze me! I
would have thought her spirit had been
invincible against all assaults of
affection.

*(enjoying Leo's dilemma then giving him another cue)*

LEONATO:
I would have sworn it had, my lord,
especially against Benedick.

*(relieved, he remembers his lines now)*

BENEDICK: *[aside]*
I should think this a gull, but that the
white-bearded fellow speaks it.

CLAUDIO: *[aside]*
He hath ta'en the infection—hold it up.

*(Xing down quickly to DP)*

DON PEDRO:
Hath she made her affection known to
Benedick?

LEONATO:
No, and swears she never will.

CLAUDIO:
It's very true, your daughter says so.
'Shall I,' she says, 'who has so often
encountered him scornfully, write to him
that I love him?'

LEONATO:
She'll get up twenty times a night, and
sit till she's written a sheet of paper—
my daughter tells us this.

CLAUDIO:
You just mentioned a sheet of paper, I
remember an amusing story that your
daughter told to us.

LEONATO:
Oh, when she'd written it and was reading
it over, she found 'Benedick' and 'Beatrice'
between the sheets?

CLAUDIO:
Yes.

LEONATO:
Oh, she tore the letter up, raged at herself
that she should be so immodest as to write
to someone that she knew would make fun of
her. 'I judge him,' she says, 'by myself
—I would make fun of him if he wrote to
me. Even though I love him, I would.'

DON PEDRO:
It would be good if Benedick learned of this
from someone else, if she won't tell him
of it.

CLAUDIO:
To what end? He'd make a joke of it and
torment the poor lady.

DON PEDRO:
She's a wonderful sweet lady, and without
question—she's virtuous.

## Act Two · Scene 3 **original abridged**

## Act Two · Scene 3 **stage directions**

LEONATO:
No, and swears she never will.

CLAUDIO:
'Tis true indeed, so your daughter says.
'Shall I,' says she, 'that have so oft
encountered him with scorn, write to him
that I love him?'

LEONATO:
She'll be up twenty times a night, and
there will she sit till she have writ
a sheet of paper—my daughter tells us.

CLAUDIO:
Now you talk of a sheet of paper, I
remember a pretty jest your daughter
told us of.

LEONATO:
O, when she writ it and was reading it
over, she found 'Benedick' and 'Beatrice'
between the sheet?

*(Cl, DP & Leo laugh, when they
stop we hear Ben still laughing
behind arbor, he stops abruptly)
('That' comes after Ben's laugh)*

CLAUDIO:
That.

LEONATO:
O, she tore the letter, railed at herself
that she should be so immodest to write
to one that she knew would flout her. 'I
measure him,' says she, 'by my own spirit—
for I should flout him if he writ to me.
Yea, though I love him, I should.'

DON PEDRO:
It were good that Benedick knew of it
by some other, if she will not discover
it.

*(DP X to UL bench, Leo & Cl
follow, DP sit L, Leo sit R,
Cl stand R of Leo, Ben climb
SL ladder to watch them)*

CLAUDIO:
To what end? He would make a sport of
it and torment the poor lady.

DON PEDRO:
She's an excellent sweet lady, and—
out of all suspicion—she is virtuous.

CLAUDIO:
And she's very wise.

DON PEDRO:
In everything but in loving Benedick.
I wish she'd fallen for me, I'd have
made her my better half. I implore you
to tell Benedick of this and hear what
he will say.

CLAUDIO:
Never tell him, my lord, let her get over
it with counseling.

LEONATO:
No, that's impossible—she'd wear her
heart out first.

DON PEDRO:
Well, let things cool down. I'm very
fond of Benedick, but I wish he would
take a good look at himself and see how
unworthy he is of such a good lady.

LEONATO:
My lord, shall we go? Dinner is ready.

CLAUDIO: *[aside]*
If he doesn't love her after this, I'll never
trust my instincts again.

DON PEDRO: *[aside]*
Let the same trap be set for her—that
must be carried out by your daughter and
her gentlewomen. Let's send her to call him
in to dinner. *[exit Don Pedro, Leonato &
Claudio]*

BENEDICK:
This can't be a trick! They bore themselves so seriously; they learned the
truth of this from Hero. They seem to
pity the lady. It appears her love is
full blown. Love me? It must be requited!
I hear what they think of me. They say
I'll act too haughty if I know she loves

CLAUDIO:
And she is exceeding wise.

DON PEDRO:
In everything but in loving Benedick.
I would she had bestowed this dotage on
me, I would have made her half myself.
I pray you tell Benedick of it and hear
what 'a will say.

*(big laugh from DP, Cl & Leo,
Ben is not amused!)*

CLAUDIO:
Never tell him, my lord, let her wear it
out with good counsel.

LEONATO:
Nay, that's impossible—she may wear her
heart out first.

DON PEDRO:
Well, let it cool the while. I love
Benedick well, and I wish he would
modestly examine himself to see how
much he is unworthy so good a lady.

LEONATO:
My lord, will you walk? Dinner is ready.

*(Leo & DP rise, X R, Cl X to
them, Ben ducks down)*

CLAUDIO: *[aside]*
If he do not dote on her upon this, I
will never trust my expectation.

DON PEDRO: *[aside]*
Let the same net be spread for her, and
that must your daughter and her gentlewomen
carry. Let us send her to call him in to
dinner. *[exit Don Pedro, Leonato &
Claudio]*

*(exit UC)*

BENEDICK:
This can be no trick! The conference was
sadly borne; they have the truth of this
from Hero. They seem to pity the lady.
It seems her affections have their full
bent. Love me? Why it must be requited!
I hear how I am censured. They say I will
bear myself proudly if I perceive the

*(straightens up and is visible
to audience again, Ben is
amazed! delivers speech from
ladder)*

me. I never thought to marry. I mustn't
be selfish. Happy is he who takes note
of his faults and corrects them. They
say the lady is fair—it's true, I
can attest to that; and virtuous—that's
so, I can't disprove it; and wise, except
for loving me—truly it's no addition
to her wit, nor any great evidence of
her folly, for I will be most dreadfully
in love with her. I may perhaps be the
object of some ridicule and some witty
attacks because I have long spoken against
marriage. But doesn't the appetite alter?
A man may love certain foods in his youth
that he cannot endure in old age. Shall
sarcasm and snide cracks and harmless
jibes deter a man's course of action?
No!—the world must be peopled. When
I said I would die a bachelor, I did
not think I would live till I were
married. Here comes Beatrice. By
gosh she's a pretty lady! I do spy some
signs of love on her.

*[enter Beatrice]*
BEATRICE:
Against my will I've been sent to ask you
to come in to dinner.

BENEDICK:
Fair Beatrice, I thank you for your trouble.

BEATRICE:
I took no more trouble for those thanks than
you took trouble to thank me. If it had been
troublesome, I would not have come.

BENEDICK:
You take pleasure then in delivering the
message?

BEATRICE:
Yes, as much as you can take at the
point of a knife. You're not hungry,
signior. Fare you well. *[exits]*

love come from her. I did never think
to marry. I must not seem proud. Happy
are they that hear their detractions
and can put them to mending. They say
the lady is fair—'tis a truth, I can
bear them witness; and virtuous—'tis
so, I cannot reprove it; and wise, but
for loving me—by my troth, it is no
addition to her wit, nor no great
argument of her folly, for I will be
horribly in love with her. I may chance
have some odd quirks and remnants of
wit broken on me because I have railed
so long against marriage. But doth not
the appetite alter? A man loves the meat
in his youth that he cannot endure in
his age. Shall quips and sentences and
these paper bullets of the brain awe a
man from the career of his humor? No!—
the world must be peopled. When I said I
would die a bachelor, I did not think I
should live till I were married. Here
comes Beatrice. By this day, she's a fair
lady! I do spy some marks of love in her.

*(Bea enters UC, X C looks around,
sees no one)*
*(Ben sighs after his line, Bea
hears this & looks up at him)*

*[enter Beatrice]*
BEATRICE:
Against my will I am sent to bid you
come in to dinner.

BENEDICK:
Fair Beatrice, I thank you for your
pains.

BEATRICE:
I took no more pains for those thanks
than you take pains to thank me. If it
had been painful, I would not have come.

*(starts to exit)*

BENEDICK:
You take pleasure then in the message?

BEATRICE:
Yea, just so much as you may take upon
a knife's point. You have no stomach,
signior. Fare you well. *[exits]*

*(stops, turns back)*

*(exits UC)*

Act Two · Scene 3      **vernacular**

BENEDICK:
Ha! 'Against my will I've been sent to ask you to come in to dinner.' There's a double meaning in that. 'I took no more trouble for those thanks than you took trouble to thank me.' That's as if to say, 'Any trouble that I take for you is as easy as thanks!' If I don't take pity on her, I'm a villain! I will go get her picture. *[exits]*

Act Three · Scene 1      **scene analysis**

    This scene parallels the previous gulling scene of Benedick, occurring this time for Beatrice's benefit. Hero and Margaret set out to surreptitiously convince Beatrice that Benedick is in love with her and is being persuaded to suffer his love in silence rather than face the disdain and scorn of Beatrice if she were to learn of it.
    Once the two ladies are convinced that they have ensnared Beatrice in their trap, they depart, allowing her to absorb this information and to commit to loving Benedick.

Act Three · Scene 1      **vernacular**

*[enter Hero, Margaret & Ursula]*
HERO:
Good Margaret, run to the parlor. There you'll find my cousin Beatrice with the Prince and Claudio. Whisper in her ear that I and Ursley are walking in the orchard and that we are talking all about her. Tell her to sneak into the arbor to hear our conversation.

MARGARET:
I'll make her come, I promise you. *[she exits]*

HERO:
Now Ursula, when Beatrice comes, our talk must only be about Benedick. When I mention his name, your part will be to praise him more than any man ever deserved. My talk to you will be how Benedick is lovesick over Beatrice. *[Beatrice enters]* Look, Beatrice is coming.

URSULA: *[aside]*
Don't worry—I know my part.

HERO: *[aside]*
Then let's go near, so that she'll miss none of this phony bait we're throwing out to her. *[aloud]* No, truly, Ursula, she is too disdainful.

| Act Two·Scene 3 **original abridged** | Act Two·Scene 3 **stage directions** |
|---|---|

BENEDICK:
Ha! 'Against my will I am sent to bid you come in to dinner.' There's a double meaning in that. 'I took no more pains for those thanks than you took pains to thank me.' That's as much to say, 'Any pains that I take for you is as easy as thanks!' If I do not take pity on her, I am a villain! I will go get her picture. *[exits]*

*(Comes down off ladder smiling ear to ear Xing DC)*

*(exits UC)*

| Act Three·Scene 1 **original abridged** | Act Three·Scene 1 **stage directions** |
|---|---|

*[enter Hero, Margaret & Ursula]*
HERO:
Good Margaret, run to the parlor. There shalt thou find my cousin Beatrice with the Prince and Claudio. Whisper her ear and tell her I and Ursley walk in the orchard and our whole discourse is all of her. Bid her steal into the bower to listen our propose.

*(Her, Mar & Ur enter DL, Her & Ur have parasols, X DLC)*

MARGARET:
I'll make her come, I warrant you. *[she exits]*

*(exit SR)*

HERO:
Now Ursula, when Beatrice doth come, our talk must only be of Benedick. When I do name him, let it be thy part to praise him more than ever man did merit. My talk to thee must be how Benedick is sick in love with Beatrice. *[Beatrice enters]* Look where Beatrice comes.

*(Xing to DL corner of stage)*

*(enter SR)*
*(facing DL, open their parasols)*

URSULA: *[aside]*
Fear you not my part of the dialogue.

*(Bea comes C, sees them, runs US & ducks behind arbor)*

HERO: *[aside]*
Then go we near her, that her ear lose nothing of the false bait we lay for it. *[aloud]* No, truly, Ursula, she is too disdainful.

*(strolling towards UR)*

URSULA:
But are you sure that Benedick loves
Beatrice so completely.

HERO:
The Prince says so and my new fiancé.

URSULA:
And did they ask you to tell her about it,
madam?

HERO:
They begged me to let her know of it;
but I persuaded them, if they loved
Benedick, to convince him to contend
with his love and never let Beatrice
know about it.

URSULA:
Why did you do that?

HERO:
Nature never created a harder heart than
that of Beatrice. Disdain and scorn sit
sparkling in her eyes, and she thinks so
much of her own wittiness that no other
subject interests her. She cannot love–
she is too self-centered.

URSULA:
I think so too; and therefore it wouldn't
be good for her to know of his love, she'd
only make fun of it.

HERO:
It's true. I've never seen a man, no
matter how wise, how noble, how young,
how good-looking, but she would tell him
off. She therefore turns every man's favors
into faults.

URSULA:
Surely, this is not commendable.

HERO:
No, to be as Beatrice is cannot be

URSULA:
But are you sure that Benedick loves
Beatrice so entirely?

*(Bea's head pops up from behind*
*arbor, she's on a ladder)*

HERO:
So says the Prince and my new-trothed lord.

*(strolling SL, Bea ducks down)*

URSULA:
And did they bid you tell her of it,
madam?

HERO:
They did entreat me to acquaint her of
it; but I persuaded them, if they loved
Benedick, to wish him wrestle with
affection and never to let Beatrice know
of it.

URSULA:
Why did you so?

*(strolling behind arbor, as*
*they approach Bea sneaks around*
*DS of arbor tiptoeing, Her &*
*Ur appear DS of arbor, sit*
*on UL bench, Bea ends up back*
*on ladder peaking over arbor)*

HERO:
Nature never framed a woman's heart of
prouder stuff than that of Beatrice.
Disdain and scorn ride sparkling in her
eyes, and her wit values itself so highly
that all matter else seems weak. She
cannot love—she is so self-endeared.

URSULA:
I think so; and therefore it were not
good she knew his love, lest she'll
make sport at it.

HERO:
You speak truth. I never yet saw man,
how wise, how noble, young, how rarely
featured, but she would spell him back-
ward. So turns she every man the wrong
side out.

URSULA:
Sure, sure it is not commendable.

HERO:
No, to be as Beatrice is cannot be

commendable. But who'd dare tell her? If
I said a word, she'd just mock me. Therefore
let Benedick waste away sighing. It'd be
better to die like that than to be ridiculed
to death.

URSULA:
Still tell her. Hear what she will say.

HERO:
No; instead I'll go to Benedick and advise
him to fight against his passion.

URSULA:
Oh, don't wrong your cousin so much!
She can't be so lacking in good sense—
having such a quick and good wit as
she's supposed to have—to refuse
so rare a gentleman as Signior
Benedick.

HERO:
Indeed he has an excellent reputation.

URSULA:
His excellent qualities earned it. When are
you to be married, madam?

HERO:
Why, tomorrow and all days after! Come, go
in. I'll show you some clothes and get your
opinion what's best to wear tomorrow.

URSULA: [aside]
She's snared, I promise you! We've caught
her, madam.

HERO: [aside]
If it turns out so, then love is determined
by fate; some people Cupid gets with his
arrows, some must be trapped with bait. [exit
Hero & Ursula]

BEATRICE:
My ears are burning. Can this be true?
Am I condemned for my haughtiness and
contemptuousness so much? Contempt

Act Three·Scene 1 **original abridged**

commendable. But who dare tell her so?
If I should speak, she would mock me.
Therefore let Benedick consume away in
sighs. It were a better death than die
with mocks.

URSULA:
Yet tell her of it. Hear what she will say.

HERO:
No; rather I will go to Benedick and
counsel him to fight against his passion.

URSULA:
O, do not do your cousin such a wrong!
She cannot be so much without true
judgment–having so swift and excellent
a wit as she is prized to have–to
refuse so rare a gentleman as Signior
Benedick.

HERO:
Indeed he hath an excellent good name.

URSULA:
His excellence did earn it. When are you
married, madam?

HERO:
Why, every day tomorrow! Come, go in.
I'll show thee some attires and have thy
counsel which is best to furnish me tomorrow.

URSULA: *[aside]*
She's limed, I warrant you! We have
caught her, madam.

HERO: *[aside]*
If it prove so, then loving goes by haps;
some Cupid kills with arrows, some with
traps. *[exit Hero & Ursula]*

BEATRICE:
What fire is in mine ears? Can this be
true? Stand I condemned for pride and
scorn so much? Contempt, farewell! And

Act Three·Scene 1 **stage directions**

*(Bea furiously nodding her head)*

*(Bea shaking her head 'no')*

*(both rise, X R)*

*(at SR)*

*(exit SR)*

*(Bea descends ladder & comes
out from behind arbor Xing C)*

### Act Three · Scene 1                vernacular

farewell! And youthful pride, adieu.
No glory is in the likes of these. And
Benedick, keep on loving—I will requite
you, and tame my wild heart to your loving
hand. If you do love, my sweetness shall
inspire you to bind our love up with a wedding
band; for it's said that you are a worthy
man and I believe it even more than I've
heard. *[exits]*

### Act Three · Scene 2        scene analysis

This scene opens with Don Pedro, Leonato, and
Claudio encountering Benedick and poking fun at
the changes that they note in him. He seems to be
sadder, is more aware of his appearance (brushing
his hat), and is wearing cologne. They determine
that these are sure-fire signs that he is in love.
Benedick, who protests that he is merely suffering
from a toothache, asks Leonato to step aside with
him so that they might talk privately. Don Pedro
guesses that Benedick wants to discuss his love for
Beatrice.

Don John enters and proceeds to put into action the plan that he and Borachio hatched in Act 2
scene 2. He tells Claudio and Don Pedro that Hero
is "disloyal." He says that they should go with him
to see her bedroom window entered the very
evening before the intended wedding. With great
reluctance, they agree to his proposal. Claudio adds
that if he sees anything to prove Don John's allegations, he will shame Hero in the very congregation
where he should have wed her.

### Act Three · Scene 2                vernacular

*[enter Don Pedro, Claudio, Benedick &
Leonato]*
DON PEDRO:
I'll remain till your wedding, and then I
go to Aragon.

CLAUDIO:
I'll escort you there, my lord, if you'll
allow me to.

DON PEDRO:
No, I will only presume on Benedick
for his company, because from the top
of his head to the sole of his foot, he
is merry.

BENEDICK:
Friends, I am not as I used to be.

LEONATO:
I agree. I think you are sadder.

CLAUDIO:
I hope he's in love.

DON PEDRO:
There's not a drop of blood in him that could
be tinged with love.

BENEDICK:
I have a toothache.

## Act Three · Scene 1  **original abridged**

maiden pride, adieu! No glory lives
behind the back of such. And Benedick,
love on—I will requite thee, taming
my wild heart to thy loving hand. If
thou dost love, my kindness shall incite
thee to bind our loves up in a holy band;
for others say thou dost deserve, and I
believe it better than reportingly.
*[exits]*

## Act Three · Scene 1  **stage directions**

*(exits UC)*

## Act Three · Scene 2  **original abridged**

*[enter Don Pedro, Claudio, Benedick &
Leonato]*
DON PEDRO:
I stay till your marriage, and then go I
toward Aragon.

CLAUDIO:
I'll bring you thither, my lord, if
you'll vouchsafe me.

DON PEDRO:
Nay, I will only be bold with Benedick
for his company, for from the crown of
his head to the sole of his foot, he is
all mirth.

BENEDICK:
Gallants, I am not as I have been.

LEONATO:
So say I. Methinks you are sadder.

CLAUDIO:
I hope he be in love.

DON PEDRO:
There's no drop of blood in him to be
truly touched with love.

BENEDICK:
I have the toothache.

## Act Three · Scene 2  **stage directions**

*(Ben enters SR with paper, sits
DR bench, reads aloud from
paper, 'the god of love, that
sits above', hears DP & Cl
talking as they approach, wads
up paper, puts it in his cheek)*
*(DP says his line from offstage)*

*(Cl starts this line offstage,
they enter UC, see Ben, X down
to him, Cl end L of Ben, DP
R of Ben, Leo behind Ben)*

*(DP, Cl & Leo laugh)*

*(slapping Ben on back)*

*(touching cheek with wad of
paper in it)*

DON PEDRO:
What? Moan about a toothache?

BENEDICK:
Well, everyone can master a grief except he who suffers it.

CLAUDIO:
Still I say, he is in love.

DON PEDRO:
There are no signs of love in him.

CLAUDIO:
If he's not in love with some woman, there's no trusting the signs. He cleans his hat every morning. What does that tell you?

DON PEDRO:
He douses himself with cologne.

CLAUDIO:
That's as much to say the sweet youth's in love.

DON PEDRO:
The greatest sign of it is his gloominess.

CLAUDIO:
And since when does he wash his face so often?

DON PEDRO:
Indeed that says it all. Conclusion, conclusion, he is in love.

BENEDICK:
Yet this is not the cure for a toothache. Old signior, walk aside with me. I have devised a little speech to say to you, that these jack-asses must not hear. *[exit Benedick & Leonato]*

DON PEDRO:
I swear, it's to talk with him about Beatrice.

DON PEDRO:
What? Sigh for the toothache?

BENEDICK:
Well, everyone can master a grief but
he that has it.

CLAUDIO:
Yet say I, he is in love.

DON PEDRO:
There is no appearance of fancy in him.

CLAUDIO:
If he be not in love with some woman,
there's no believing old signs. 'A
brushes his hat o' mornings. What should
that bode?

*(taking Ben's hat off his head
& tossing it to DP)*

DON PEDRO:
'A rubs himself with civit.

*(sniffing Ben's ear)*

CLAUDIO:
That's as much as to say the sweet
youth's in love.

*(sniffing Ben's other ear, Ben
rises, X DLC, DP & Cl follow)*

DON PEDRO:
The greatest note of it is his melancholy.

CLAUDIO:
And when was he wont to wash his face?

DON PEDRO:
Indeed that tells a heavy tale. Conclude,
conclude, he is in love.

*(puts hat back on Ben's head)*

BENEDICK:
Yet is this no charm for the toothache.
Old signior, walk aside with me. I have
studied eight or nine wise words to
speak to you, which these hobby-horses
must not hear. *[exit Benedick & Leonato]*

*(Xing to Leo)*

*(exit SR)*

DON PEDRO:
For my life, to break with him about
Beatrice.

*(DP & Cl X & sit on UL bench,
Cl L of DP)*

*[enter Don John]*
DON JOHN:
My lord and brother, God save you!

DON PEDRO:
Good evening, brother.

DON JOHN:
If you've a moment, I have something to say to you.

DON PEDRO:
In private?

DON JOHN:
If you wouldn't mind. Yet Count Claudio might like to hear, for what I have to say concerns him.

DON PEDRO:
What is it?

DON JOHN: *[to Claudio]*
Does your lordship intend to be married tomorrow?

DON PEDRO:
You know he does.

DON JOHN:
I don't know that, when he knows what I know.

CLAUDIO:
If there be any impediment, I beg you to reveal it.

DON JOHN:
I came here to tell you—the lady is disloyal.

CLAUDIO:
Who, Hero?

DON JOHN:
Even she—Leonato's Hero, your Hero, everyman's Hero.

| Act Three · Scene 2 **original abridged** | Act Three · Scene 2    **stage directions** |
| --- | --- |
| *[enter Don John]* | *(enter SL, X L of bench)* |
| DON JOHN: | |
| My lord and brother, God save you! | |
| | |
| DON PEDRO: | |
| Good den, brother. | |
| | |
| DON JOHN: | |
| If your leisure served, I would speak | |
| with you. | |
| | |
| DON PEDRO: | |
| In private? | |
| | |
| DON JOHN: | *(Cl rise, X R of DP as if to* |
| If it please you. Yet Count Claudio may | *go, Cl stops & turns back)* |
| hear, for what I would speak of concerns | |
| him. | |
| | |
| DON PEDRO: | |
| What's the matter? | |
| | |
| DON JOHN: *[to Claudio]* | *(Xing between DP & Cl)* |
| Means your lordship to be married | |
| tomorrow? | |
| | |
| DON PEDRO: | |
| You know he does. | |
| | |
| DON JOHN: | |
| I know not that, when he knows what I | |
| know. | |
| | |
| CLAUDIO: | |
| If there be any impediment, I pray you | |
| discover it. | |
| | |
| DON JOHN: | |
| I came hither to tell you—the lady is | |
| disloyal. | |
| | |
| CLAUDIO: | |
| Who, Hero? | |
| | |
| DON JOHN: | |
| Even she—Leonato's Hero, your Hero, | |
| everyman's Hero. | |

CLAUDIO:
Disloyal?

DON JOHN:
The word is too good to fully express her wickedness. Think up a worse title and I will use it on her. Go with me tonight, you shall see her bedroom window entered, even on the night before her wedding day. If you still love her then, wed her tomorrow, but it would serve your honor better to change your mind.

CLAUDIO:
Can this be so?

DON PEDRO:
I won't even think it.

DON JOHN:
If you doubt what you see, say nothing about it. If you will follow me, I'll show you sufficient proof; and when you've seen it and heard it, proceed accordingly.

CLAUDIO:
If I see anything tonight why I should not marry her tomorrow, in the congregation where I should wed, there I will shame her.

DON PEDRO:
And just as I helped you to win her, I will join with you to disgrace her.

DON JOHN:
Maintain your composure till midnight and then see it all for yourself.

DON PEDRO:
Oh what a day this has turned out to be!

CLAUDIO:
Oh what strange mischief is in the air!

| Act Three · Scene 2 **original abridged** | Act Three · Scene 2 **stage directions** |
|---|---|

CLAUDIO:
Disloyal?

DON JOHN:
The word is too good to paint out her wickedness. Think you of a worse title and I will fit her to it. Go with me tonight, you shall see her chamber-window entered, even the night before her wedding-day. If you love her then, tomorrow wed her, but it would better fit your honor to change your mind.

CLAUDIO:
May this be so?

DON PEDRO:
I will not think it.                                    *(rising)*

DON JOHN:
If you dare not trust that you see, confess not that you know. If you will follow me, I will show you enough; and when you have seen more and heard more, proceed accordingly.

CLAUDIO:
If I see anything tonight why I should not marry her tomorrow, in the congregation where I should wed, there will I shame her.

DON PEDRO:
And as I wooed for thee to obtain her, I will join with thee to disgrace her.

DON JOHN:
Bear it coldly but till midnight and let the issue show itself.

DON PEDRO:
O day untowardly turned!

CLAUDIO:
O mischief strangely thwarting!

**DON JOHN:**
Oh what a disaster is prevented! That is what you shall say when you've seen what you shall see. *[they exit]*

Act Three • Scene 3    **scene analysis**

Here we meet Dogberry and Verges, the law enforcement wing of Messina. They are in the process of assembling and training their team of night watchmen for the evening's work.

They determine that George Seacoal shall head the Watch because of his reading and writing skills. They go on to give the men their orders, noting that they should pay particular attention to Leonato's house due to the wedding being there tomorrow.

Dogberry and Verges depart, and Borachio and Conrade enter. Borachio drunkenly tells Conrade about the part he played in the deception of Claudio and Don Pedro concerning Hero.

The Watch, realizing that this is a "dangerous piece of lechery," arrests them both.

**"Rightly reasoned, and in his own division"**
A DICTIONARY TO DECIPHER DOGBERRYISMS

Dogberry's intense desire to move up the social ladder exhibits itself in his use of language. He, like many others, thinks that using fancy words will make him appear smarter and more upper class. So whenever possible, Dogberry will throw the biggest word he can think of into the conversation. Sometimes, he'll pick a word that is vaguely similar to the correct one; other times he is way off the mark.

Verges obviously talks and understands "Dogberry," and the Watch pick it up pretty fast. See the "Dogberry Dictionary" at the beginning of each of their scenes to decipher the underlined words.

| *When Dogberry or his cohorts say:* | *What they really mean is:* |
| --- | --- |
| salvation | damnation |
| desartless | deserving |
| by nature | by hard work |
| senseless | sensible |

Act Three • Scene 3    **vernacular**

*[enter Dogberry, Verges & the Watch]*
**DOGBERRY:**
Are you good men and true?

**VERGES:**
Yep, or else they would suffer <u>salvation</u>, body and soul.

**DOGBERRY:**
Nope, that'd be too good a punishment for them, having been chosen as the Prince's watchmen.

**VERGES:**
Well, give them their orders, neighbor Dogberry.

**DOGBERRY:**
First, who do you think is the most <u>desartless</u> man to be the head watch?

**FIRST WATCH:**
George Seacoal, 'cause he can write and read.

**DOGBERRY:**
Come here, neighbor Seacoal. God has blessed you—to be handsome is the gift of fortune, but to write and read comes <u>by nature</u>.

**SECOND WATCH:**
Both of which, Master Constable—

**DOGBERRY:** *[interrupting]*
You have. I knew that would be your answer. You are thought to be the most

**Act Three · Scene 2 original abridged**

DON JOHN:
O plague right well prevented! So will
you say when you have seen the sequel.
*[they exit]*

**Act Three · Scene 2    stage directions**

*(exit SR)*

**Act Three · Scene 3 original abridged**

*[enter Dogberry, Verges & the Watch]*
DOGBERRY:
Are you good men and true?

VERGES:
Yea, or else they should suffer <u>salvation</u>,
body and soul.

DOGBERRY:
Nay, that were a punishment too good
for them, being chosen for the Prince's
watch.

VERGES:
Well, give them their charge, neighbor
Dogberry.

DOGBERRY:
First, who think you the most <u>desartless</u>
man to be constable?

FIRST WATCH:
George Seacoal, for he can write and read.

DOGBERRY:
Come hither, neighbor Seacoal. God hath
blest you—to be a well-favored man is
the gift of fortune, but to write and
read comes <u>by nature</u>.

SECOND WATCH:
Both which, Master Constable—

DOGBERRY: *[interrupting]*
You have. I knew that would be your
answer. You are thought here to be the

**Act Three · Scene 3    stage directions**

*(enter DL, Dog, W1, W2 & Ver,
Ver has lantern, Xing to DC,
standing in a semi-circle,
Dog is SR, W1 R of W2, Ver
is SL)*

*(pointing to W2)*

*(Dog X DS a step, W2 X to Dog)*

| Act Three · Scene 3 | scene analysis |
|---|---|
| *Cont.* | |
| comprehend | apprehend |
| vagrom | vagrant |
| tolerable | intolerable |
| vigitant | vigilant |
| lechery | treachery |

**Act Three · Scene 3        vernacular**

<u>senseless</u> and fit man to be the head of the watch. Therefore you carry the lantern. These are your orders—you shall <u>comprehend</u> all <u>vagrom</u> men; you are to tell any man, 'Halt, in the Prince's name.'

SECOND WATCH:
What if he won't halt?

DOGBERRY:
Why then, ignore him, and let him go and thank God you are rid of a rascal.

VERGES:
If he won't halt when he's told, he's not a loyal subject of the Prince.

DOGBERRY:
True, and they are to meddle with none but the Prince's subjects. You shall also make no noise in the streets—for the watch to babble and talk is most <u>tolerable</u> and should not be endured.

FIRST WATCH:
We would rather sleep than talk; we know what's expected of a watch.

DOGBERRY:
Why you sound like a traditional and very quiet watchman, for I can't see how sleeping should offend. You are to look in at all the bars and tell those who are drunk to get to bed.

SECOND WATCH:
How if they won't?

DOGBERRY:
Why then, let them alone till they sober up. If you come upon a thief, you may suspect him to be a dishonest man; and for this type of men, the less you mess with them, the better.

## Act Three · Scene 3 **original abridged**

most <u>senseless</u> and fit man for the
constable of the watch. Therefore bear
you the lantern. This is your charge—
you shall <u>comprehend</u> all <u>vagrom</u> men; you
are to bid any man stand, in the Prince's
name.

SECOND WATCH:
How if a will not stand?

DOGBERRY:
Why then, take no note of him, but let
him go and thank God you are rid of a knave.

VERGES:
If he will not stand when he is bidden,
he is none of the Prince's subjects.

DOGBERRY:
True, and they are to meddle with none
but the Prince's subjects. You shall also
make no noise in the streets—for the
watch to babble and talk is most <u>tolerable</u>
and not to be endured.

FIRST WATCH:
We will rather sleep than talk; we know
what belongs to a watch.

DOGBERRY:
Why you speak like an ancient and most
quiet watchman, for I cannot see how
sleeping should offend. You are to call
at all ale-houses and bid those that are
drunk get them to bed.

SECOND WATCH:
How if they will not?

DOGBERRY:
Why then, let them alone til they are
sober. If you meet a thief, you may
suspect him to be no true man; and for
such kind of men, the less you meddle
with them the more is your honesty.

## Act Three · Scene 3   **stage directions**

*(Ver X to L of W2, hand lantern
to him, Ver & Dog shake W2's
hand, all return to original
positions for 'this is your
charge')*

*(X up & around W1, end between
W1 & W2, puts hands on their
shoulders)*

**Act Three • Scene 3          vernacular**

SECOND WATCH:
If we're sure he's a thief, shouldn't we
arrest him?

DOGBERRY:
Truly, according to the law you may—but
I think, if you lay down with dogs, you'll
get up with fleas. If you come upon a thief,
let him show his true colors and steal away
from you.

VERGES:
You have always been called a merciful man,
partner.

DOGBERRY:
Truly.

VERGES:
If you hear a child crying in the night,
you must call to the nurse and tell her to
quiet it.

FIRST WATCH:
How if the nurse is asleep and doesn't
hear us?

DOGBERRY:
Why then leave quietly and let the
child wake her with its crying. This
ends your orders. Well, men, good
night. If anything important should
happen, wake me up. Good night. Come
neighbor.

SECOND WATCH:
Well, we have our orders. Let's go sit on
the church bench till two, and then go to
bed.

DOGBERRY:
One more word, honest neighbors. You must
watch around Signior Leonato's house, 'cause
since the wedding is there tomorrow, there's
lots going on there tonight. Adieu, Be
vigitant. *[exit Dogberry & Verges]*

Act Three · Scene 3 **original abridged**

Act Three · Scene 3    **stage directions**

SECOND WATCH:
If we know him to be a thief, shall we
not lay hands on him?

DOGBERRY:
Truly, by your office you may—but I
think they that touch pitch are defiled.
If you do take a thief, let him show
himself what he is and steal out of your
company.

VERGES:
You have always been called a merciful
man, partner.

DOGBERRY:
Truly.

VERGES:
If you hear a child cry in the night,
you must call to the nurse and bid her
still it.

FIRST WATCH:
How if the nurse be asleep and will not
hear us?

DOGBERRY:
Why then depart in peace and let the
child wake her with crying. This is the
end of the charge. Well, masters, good
night. And there be any matter of weight        *(Dog starts Xing DS of them*
chances, call up me. Good night. Come       *to DL, stops, turns back)*
neighbor.                                                          *(Dog exits DL, Ver follows)*

SECOND WATCH:
Well, we hear our charge. Let us go sit       *(W2 & W1 X to DR bench, sit)*
here upon the church bench till two, and
then to bed.

DOGBERRY:
One word more, honest neighbors. I pray    *(Dog reenters DL, Ver following,*
you watch about Signior Leonato's door,     *X DC, Watch rise quickly)*
for the wedding being there tomorrow,
there is a great coil tonight. Adieu. Be
<u>vigitant</u>. *[exit Dogberry & Verges]*                *(exit DL)*

**Act Three · Scene 3          vernacular**

*[enter Borachio & Conrade]*
BORACHIO:
Hey, Conrade!

SECOND WATCH: *[aside]*
Hush! Don't move!

BORACHIO:
Conrade, hey man!

CONRADE:
I'm here man. Right next to you.

BORACHIO:
Stay close then and I'll—just like a true
drunkard—tell you everything.

SECOND WATCH: *[aside]*
Something's up; stand by.

BORACHIO:
Let me tell you, I have earned a thousand
gold coins from Don John.

CONRADE:
Is it possible that villainy should cost
so much?

BORACHIO:
When rich villains have need of poor ones,
poor ones may set whatever price they dare.

SECOND WATCH: *[aside]*
He's a vile thief.

BORACHIO:
Did you hear somebody?

CONRADE:
No, it was only the weathervane on the house.

BORACHIO:
I'll tell you—tonight I wooed Margaret,
Lady Hero's gentlewoman, by the name
'Hero.' She leans out of her mistress'
bedroom window, tells me 'a thousand
times good night'—I'm telling this

| Act Three · Scene 3 **original abridged** | Act Three · Scene 3 **stage directions** |
| --- | --- |

*[enter Borachio & Conrade]*
BORACHIO:
What, Conrade!

                *(Bor appears atop SR ladder)*

SECOND WATCH: *[aside]*
Peace! Stir not!

                *(Watch turn bench 90° & duck behind it, peaking out to observe)*

BORACHIO:
Conrade, I say!

CONRADE:
Here, man. I am at thy elbow.

                *(Con appears atop SL ladder)*

BORACHIO:
Stand thee close then and I will—like
a true drunkard—utter all to thee.

SECOND WATCH: *[aside]*
Some treason; stand close.

BORACHIO:
Know, I have earned of Don John a
thousand ducats.

CONRADE:
Is it possible that any villainy should
be so dear?

BORACHIO:
When rich villains have need of poor ones,
poor ones may make what price they will.

SECOND WATCH: *[aside]*
A vile thief.

BORACHIO:
Didst thou not hear somebody?

                *(they descend ladders, come around arbor to C, look around)*

CONRADE:
No, 'twas the vane on the house.

BORACHIO:
Know that I have tonight wooed Margaret,
the Lady Hero's gentlewoman, by the name
of Hero. She leans me out at her mistress'
chamber window, bids me a thousand times
good night—I tell this tale vilely—I

                *(Bor & Con X to SL bench, sit, Bor US of Con)*

tale vilely—I should've first told
you how the Prince, Claudio, and my
master, Don John, saw this charming
encounter from far off in the orchard.

CONRADE:
And did they think Margaret was Hero?

BORACHIO:
Two of them did, the Prince and Claudio.
But that devil, my master, knew she was
Margaret; and partly due to his vowing to
it; partly because of the dark night, but
chiefly because of my wickedness, Claudio
went away enraged swearing that he would
meet her the next morning at the temple and
there, before the whole congregation, shame
her, and send her home without a husband.

SECOND WATCH:
We charge you in the Prince's name,
halt!

FIRST WATCH:
Wake up the Master Constable; we have here
the most dangerous bit of <u>lechery</u> that's
ever been known in the commonwealth.

CONRADE:
Masters, masters—

SECOND WATCH:
Don't speak, we order you—go with us.
*[they exit]*

Act Three·Scene 4      **scene analysis**

It is the morning of the wedding, and Margaret
is helping Hero to prepare for the upcoming event
and kidding her all the while. Beatrice, who has
been sent for, arrives on the scene sounding as
though she has a cold.

Margaret and Hero, who obviously believe the
cold to be a sign of the lovesickness, which Beatrice

Act Three·Scene 4      **vernacular**

*[enter Hero, Margaret & Ursula]*
HERO:
Good Ursula, wake my cousin Beatrice.

URSULA:
I will, lady.

Act Three · Scene 3 **original abridged**

should first tell thee how the Prince, Claudio, and my master, Don John, saw afar off in the orchard this amiable encounter.

CONRADE:
And thought they Margaret was Hero?

BORACHIO:
Two of them did, the Prince and Claudio. But the devil, my master, knew she was Margaret; and partly by his oaths, partly by the dark night, but chiefly by my villainy, away went Claudio enraged; swore he would meet her next morning at the temple and there, before the whole congregation, shame her, and send her home without a husband.

SECOND WATCH:
We charge you in the Prince's name, stand!

FIRST WATCH:
Call up the Master Constable; we have here the most dangerous piece of lechery that ever was known in the commonwealth.

CONRADE:
Masters, masters—

SECOND WATCH:
Never speak, we charge you—go with us.
[they exit]

Act Three · Scene 3   **stage directions**

*(Watch jump up, Con jumps up, Bor has to be helped by Con)*

*(Watch X to Bor & Con, who run, there is a chase around the arbor, appropriate ad libs)*

*(Watch catch them, take them off DL)*

Act Three · Scene 4 **original abridged**

[enter Hero, Margaret & Ursula]
HERO:
Good Ursula, wake my cousin Beatrice.

URSULA
I will, lady.

Act Three · Scene 4   **stage directions**

*(enter SR, Ur turns bench back, Her sits holds up mirror, Mar puts veil & gloves on bench, stands behind Her, brushes Her's hair)*

| Act Three·Scene 4    **scene analysis** | Act Three·Scene 4    **vernacular** |
|---|---|

*Cont.*
is now in the throes of, proceed to taunt her. Margaret suggests that she take carduus benedictus, which is an herbal remedy for illness but, more importantly, sounds like "Benedick."

Margaret then announces that the gentlemen are arriving to escort Hero to the church, and the scene ends with the ladies helping Hero to finish dressing.

HERO:
And ask her to come here. *[Ursula exits]*

MARGARET:
Your gown's extraordinarily fashioned. I've seen the Duchess of Milan's gown that's been so highly praised.

HERO:
Oh, that's exceptional, they say.

MARGARET:
Indeed, it's just a night gown compared to yours—yours is worth ten of it.

HERO:
God give me joy to wear it, for my heart is very heavy.

MARGARET:
It'll be heavier soon with the weight of a man.

HERO:
Darn you, aren't you ashamed?

MARGARET:
Of what, lady? Of speaking honorably? Isn't marriage honorable? Isn't your fiance honorable? I offend nobody. Is there any harm in saying 'heavier with a husband'? None I think if it's the right husband and the right wife. Ask my Lady Beatrice—here she comes. *[enter Beatrice]*

HERO:
Good morning, coz.

BEATRICE: *[sounding sickly]*
Good morning, sweet Hero.

HERO:
Why, what's the matter? Are you tuning up with a cold?

BEATRICE:
I haven't got any other tune, I think.

**HERO:**
And bid her come hither. *[Ursula exits]*

**MARGARET:**
Your gown's a most rare fashion, i' faith.
I saw the Duchess of Milan's gown that
they praise so.

**HERO:**
O, that exceeds, they say.

**MARGARET:**
By my troth, 's but a nightgown in respect
of yours—yours is worth ten on't.

**HERO:**
God give me joy to wear it, for my heart
is exceeding heavy.

**MARGARET:**
'Twill be heavier soon by the weight of
a man.

**HERO:**
Fie upon thee, art not ashamed?

**MARGARET:**
Of what, lady? Of speaking honorably? Is
not marriage honorable? Is not your lord
honorable? I offend nobody. Is there any
harm in 'heavier for a husband'? None I
think, and it be the right husband and
the right wife. Ask my Lady Beatrice—
here she comes. *[enter Beatrice]*

**HERO:**
Good morrow, coz.

**BEATRICE:** *[sounding sickly]*
Good morrow, sweet Hero.

**HERO:**
Why, how now? Do you speak in the sick
tune?

**BEATRICE:**
I am out of all other tune, methinks.

*(Ur exits UR)*

*(jumps up, playfully chases
Mar L, returns & sits)*

*(Xing back during speech to
L of bench)*

*(offstage sneeze from Bea)*
*(enter UR)*

*(at UR entrance)*

It's almost five o'clock, cousin, it's
time you were ready. Truly, I am
very ill.

HERO:
These gloves that the Count sent me are
wonderfully perfumed.

BEATRICE:
I'm stuffed up, cousin, I can't smell.

MARGARET:
A maiden and stuffed up! That's a good way
to catch a cold.

BEATRICE:
Oh, God help me! God, help me!

MARGARET:
Aren't I amazingly witty?

BEATRICE:
You should try using it more often. Oh truly,
I am sick.

MARGARET:
Try some of that distilled <u>carduus</u>
<u>benedictus</u>*, and place it on your heart.
It's the best thing for a cold.

*(\*Carduus benedictus was a common
herbal remedy of the time.)*

HERO: *[whispering to Margaret]*
You've pricked her with a thorn.

BEATRICE:
Benedictus! Why benedictus? You have some
hidden meaning in this benedictus.

MARGARET:
Hidden meaning? No, truly, I have no hidden
meaning; I mean plain holy thistle. Maybe
you think, I think that you're in love. No,
I'm not so dumb to think that you are in
love, or that you ever will be in love, or
that you are even capable of being in love.
Yet Benedick was like that. He swore he'd
never marry; and yet now, in spite of his

'Tis almost five o'clock, cousin, 'tis
time you were ready. By my troth, I am
exceeding ill!

HERO:
These gloves the Count sent me, they are
an excellent perfume.

BEATRICE:
I am stuffed, cousin, I cannot smell.

MARGARET:
A maid and stuffed! There's goodly
catching of cold.

BEATRICE:
O, God help me! God, help me!

MARGARET:
Doth not my wit become me rarely?

BEATRICE:
It is not seen enough. By my troth,
I am sick.

MARGARET:
Get you some of this distilled <u>carduus
benedictus</u>,* and lay it to your heart.
It is the only thing for a qualm.

HERO: *[whispering to Margaret]*
Thou prick'st her with a thistle.

BEATRICE:
Benedictus! Why benedictus? You have some
moral in this benedictus.

MARGARET:
Moral? No, by my troth, I have no moral
meaning; I meant plain holy thistle. You
may think perchance that I think you are
in love. Nay, I am not such a fool to think
that you are in love, or that you will be
in love, or that you can be in love. Yet
Benedick was such another. He swore he
would never marry; and yet now, in despite

*(Xing to behind bench, takes
brush from Mar, brushes Her's
hair)*

*(holding gloves to Bea's nose)*

*(Mar X R infront of Her & sit
R of Her)*

*(cupping her hand to Mar's ear)*

*(X DR of bench, threatening
Mar with hairbrush)*

*(Mar rise, back up & around
bench as Bea pursues her during
this speech)*

hard-hearted vow, he's taking his medicine like a man. That you could change your mind —I don't know, but I think you're as human as other women are.

BEATRICE:
Doesn't your mouth ever stop?

*[enter Ursula]*
URSULA:
Madam, come on! The Prince, the Count, Signior Benedick, Don John, and all the noblemen of the town have come to escort you to church.

HERO:
Help me to dress, dear coz, good Meg, good Ursula. *[they exit]*

Act Three·Scene 5   **scene analysis**

Dogberry and Verges arrive at Leonato's house to inform him of the arrests of Borachio and Conrade. Leonato is in such haste getting ready for the wedding that he dismisses them, telling them to question the prisoners themselves.

*Dogberry Dictionary*

| | |
|---|---|
| confidence | conference |
| decerns | concerns |
| blunt | sharp |
| comprehended | apprehended |
| aspicious | suspicious |
| suffigance | sufficient |
| examination | examine |

Act Three·Scene 5          **vernacular**

*[enter Leonato, Dogberry & Verges]*
LEONATO:
What do you want with me, honest neighbor.

DOGBERRY:
Truly, sir, to have a <u>confidence</u> with you about something that <u>decerns</u> you personally.

LEONATO:
Be brief, please, you can see it's a busy time for me.

DOGBERRY:
Truly, this is it, sir.

VERGES:
Yes, truly it is, sir.

LEONATO:
What is it, my good friends?

DOGBERRY:
Good Verges, sir, gets a little off the track—he's an old man, sir, and his

of his heart, he eats his meat without grudging. How you may be converted I know not, but methinks you look with your eyes as other women do.

*(Mar end back up in DR corner, Bea facing her, holding hairbrush up)*

BEATRICE:
What pace is this that thy tongue keeps?

*[enter Ursula]*
URSULA:
Madam, withdraw! The Prince, the Count, Signior Benedick, Don John and all the gallants of the town are come to fetch you to church

*(Ur enters SR, stops)*

HERO:
Help to dress me, good coz, good Meg, good Ursula. *[they exit]*

*(Mar grabs veil, Her takes gloves & mirror, UR X to bench & moves it to DR side of stage, all exit SR)*

*[enter Leonato, Dogberry & Verges]*
LEONATO:
What would you with me, honest neighbor?

*(Leo enters UC, heading SR, in a hurry, Dog & Ver follow)*

DOGBERRY:
Marry, sir, I would have some <u>confidence</u> with you that <u>decerns</u> you nearly.

LEONATO:
Brief, I pray you, for you see it is a busy time with me.

*(stops RC, turns to them)*

DOGBERRY:
Marry, this it is, sir.

VERGES:
Yes, in truth it is, sir.

LEONATO:
What is it, my good friends?

DOGBERRY:
Good Verges, sir, speaks a little off the matter—an old man, sir, and his

*(Dog takes Leo DS a step, talking confidentially)*

wits are not as <u>blunt as</u>, dear God, I
wish they were, but, believe me, he's
honest.

VERGES:
Yes, I thank God, I am as honest as any
man living—who is an old man—and no
honester than I.

LEONATO:
I must leave you.

DOGBERRY:
One word sir. Our watch, sir, have
<u>comprehended</u> two <u>aspicious</u> persons and we
would like to examine them in your honor's
presence.

LEONATO:
Take the examination yourself and bring it
to me. I'm in a great hurry, as you can
plainly see.

DOGBERRY:
It shall be <u>suffigance</u>.

LEONATO:
Fare you well. *[exits]*

DOGBERRY:
Go partner, get the Sexton, ask him to bring
his pen and inkwell to the jail—we are
now to <u>examination</u> these men.

VERGES:
We must do it wisely.

DOGBERRY:
We won't be short of wits, I promise you.
*[they exit]*

wits are not so <u>blunt</u> as, God help, I
would desire they were, but, in faith,
honest.

VERGES:
Yes, I thank God, I am as honest as any
man living—that is an old man—and
no honester than I.

*(Xing D to them)*

LEONATO:
I must leave you.

*(starts to leave)*

DOGBERRY:
One word sir. Our watch, sir, have
<u>comprehended</u> two <u>aspicious</u> persons and
we would have them this morning examined
before your worship.

*(Leo stops & turns back)*

LEONATO:
Take their examination yourself and bring
it me. I am now in great haste, as it may
appear unto you.

DOGBERRY:
It shall be <u>suffigance</u>.

LEONATO:
Fare you well. *[exits]*

*(exits SR)*

DOGBERRY:
Go partner, get the Sexton, bid him bring
his pen and inkhorn to the jail—we are
now to <u>examination</u> these men.

*(Xing DL)*

VERGES:
We must do it wisely.

DOGBERRY:
We will spare for no wit, I warrant you.
*[they exit]*

*(exit DL)*

This is the wedding scene and Friar Francis is attempting to perform the ceremony. Claudio seems to be presenting various obstacles, and it finally comes out that he is rejecting Hero and accusing her of being a slut.

Claudio wants to question Hero and asks Leonato to insist that she answer truthfully. Leonato does so, and Claudio asks Hero what man she talked to last night out of her bedroom window. When Hero insists that she spoke to no man, Don Pedro tells the congregation that he, his brother, and Claudio all witnessed her talking with "a ruffian at her chamber window."

Hero faints and her accusers go off leaving the shocked assembly behind. Benedick and Beatrice show concern for Hero, but Leonato wishes his daughter dead.

When Beatrice, who had shared a room with Hero for the past year, admits that she slept elsewhere last night, Leonato is convinced the accusation against his daughter is true.

Friar Francis intervenes, saying that he has been observing Hero's reactions and that in his eyes they show her to be innocent and that her accusers must be mistaken. Benedick deduces that if this is true, Don John, the bastard, is the man behind all this trouble.

Leonato says he would personally kill his daughter if what has been said about her is true, but if it is false, he would make the liars pay for it.

Friar Francis suggests that they put out the word that Hero died as a result of the accusation. This should give events time to straighten themselves out. Leonato agrees to this, and all depart leaving Beatrice and Benedick alone in the church.

Benedick notices that Beatrice has been crying, and he tells her that he believes Hero to be innocent. Beatrice says she wishes she knew a man who would defend Hero's honor for her.

Benedick tells Beatrice that he loves her, and when she professes her love for him, he offers to do anything for her. She tells him to "Kill Claudio!" His response is "Ha! Not for the wide world!" Beatrice starts to leave but Benedick stops her. She passionately defends her cousin's innocence and convinces Benedick to prove his love by challenging Claudio to a duel.

*[enter Don Pedro, Don John, Leonato, Friar Francis, Claudio, Benedick, Hero, Beatrice & Antonio]*

LEONATO:
Come on, Friar Francis, be brief.

FRIAR FRANCIS:
You've come here, my lord, to marry this lady?

CLAUDIO:
No.

LEONATO:
To be married to her, friar—you come to marry her.

FRIAR FRANCIS:
Lady, do you come here to be married to this Count?

HERO:
I do.

FRIAR FRANCIS:
If either of you know any impediment why you should not be joined, I instruct you— on your souls to speak it.

CLAUDIO:
Do you know any Hero?

HERO:
None, my lord.

FRIAR FRANCIS:
Do you know any, Count?

LEONATO:
I dare to answer for him—none.

CLAUDIO:
Oh, what men dare do!—not knowing what they do!

BENEDICK:
What's this? Wisecracks?

*[enter Don Pedro, Don John, Leonato,
Friar Francis, Claudio, Benedick, Hero,
Beatrice & Antonio]*
LEONATO:
Come, Friar Francis, be brief.

FRIAR FRANCIS:
You come hither, my lord, to marry this
lady?

CLAUDIO:
No.

LEONATO:
To be married to her, friar—you come to
marry her.

FRIAR FRANCIS:
Lady, you come hither to be married to
this Count?

HERO:
I do.

FRIAR FRANCIS:
If either of you know any impediment why
you should not be joined, I charge you
on your souls to utter it.

CLAUDIO:
Know you any, Hero?

HERO:
None, my lord.

FRIAR FRANCIS:
Know you any, Count?

LEONATO:
I dare make his answer—none.

CLAUDIO:
O, what men dare do!—not knowing what
they do!

BENEDICK:
How now? Interjections?

*(FF enters UC, X to C, there are 2 lines
behind him, on R, Leo, Ant, Bea & Her, on
L, DP, DJ, Ben & Cl, Leo & DP X to DR &
DL of FF, Ant & DJ X to DR & DL of Leo &
DP, Bea & Ben X to DR & DL of Ant & DJ,
Her & Cl X to DR & DL of Bea & Ben, Her has
veil, gloves & bouquet)*
*(Her & Cl X to DS of FF, kneel
facing each other)*

*(Ben, Bea, Ant, Leo, Her & FF
laugh)*

CLAUDIO:
Just a minute, friar. *[to Leonato]* Father,
do you freely and with a clear conscience
give me this maiden, your daughter?

LEONATO:
As freely, son, as God gave her to me.

CLAUDIO:
And what do I have to give to you that
could equal this rare and precious gift?

DON PEDRO:
Nothing, unless you give her back again.

CLAUDIO:
Sweet Prince, you teach me gratitude.
There, Leonato, take her back again.
Don't give this rotten apple to your
friend. Observe her virginal blushes!
Doesn't that blush seem to indicate
her innocence? Wouldn't you swear,
all of you who see her, that she looks
like a maiden? But she is not. She
knows the passions of a lascivious
bed. Her blush is guiltiness, not
modesty.

LEONATO:
What do you mean, my lord?

CLAUDIO:
Not to be married! Not to enmesh my soul
to a proven slut.

LEONATO:
My dear lord, if you have conquered
her youthful resistance and taken her
virginity—

CLAUDIO:
I know what you would say. If I have
slept with her, you'd say she took me
as a husband, and that would excuse
any sin. No, Leonato, I never tempted

CLAUDIO:
Stand thee by, friar. *[to Leonato]* Father, will you with free and unconstrained soul give me this maid, your daughter?

LEONATO:
As freely, son, as God did give her me.

CLAUDIO:
And what have I to give you back whose worth may counterpoise this rich and precious gift?

DON PEDRO:
Nothing, unless you render her again.

CLAUDIO:
Sweet Prince, you learn me thankfulness. There, Leonato, take her back again. Give not this rotten orange to your friend. Behold how like a maid she blushes! Comes not that blood as modest evidence to witness simple virtue? Would you not swear, all you that see her, that she were a maid by these exterior shows? But she is none. She knows the heat of a luxurious bed. Her blush is guiltiness, not modesty.

LEONATO:
What do you mean, my lord?

CLAUDIO:
Not to be married! Not to knit my soul to an approved wanton.

LEONATO:
Dear my lord, if you have vanquished the resistance of her youth and made defeat of her virginity—

CLAUDIO:
I know what you would say. If I have known her, you will say she did embrace me as a husband, and so extenuate the sin. No, Leonato, I never tempted her

*(rises, helps Her get up)*

*(X to R of Her)*

*(shoves Her into Leo's arms)*

*(Xing DL a little)*

*(letting go of Her, taking a step DS)*

*(Xing DL of Her)*

her but acted only with bashful sincerity
and appropriate love.

HERO:
And did I ever seem otherwise to you?

CLAUDIO:
Damn your seeming! You seem to me as
innocent as a bud before it blooms,
but you are more lustful than those
animals that seethe with savage sensuality.

HERO:
Are you well, my lord, that you talk like this?

LEONATO:
Sweet Prince, why don't you say something?

DON PEDRO:
What should I say? I stand here dishonored
for having attempted to join my dear friend
to a common whore.

LEONATO:
Are these things spoken, or am I
dreaming?

DON JOHN:
Sir, they are spoken, and these things
are true.

BENEDICK:
This doesn't look like a wedding.

HERO:
'True?' Oh God!

CLAUDIO:
Leonato, let me pose one question to
your daughter. And by your fatherly
influence over her, tell her to
answer truthfully.

LEONATO:
I order you to do so.

but showed bashful sincerity and comely
love.

HERO:
And seemed I ever otherwise to you?

CLAUDIO:
Out on the seeming! You seem to me as
chaste as is the bud ere it be blown,
but you are more intemperate in your
blood than those animals that rage in
savage sensuality.

HERO:
Is my lord well that he doth speak so?

LEONATO:
Sweet Prince, why speak not you?

DON PEDRO:
What should I speak? I stand dishonored
that have gone about to link my dear
friend to a common stale.

LEONATO:
Are these things spoken, or do I but
dream?

DON JOHN:
Sir, they are spoken, and these things
are true.

BENEDICK:
This looks not like a nuptial.

HERO:
'True?' O God!

CLAUDIO:
Leonato, let me but move one question
to your daughter. And by that fatherly
power that you have in her, bid her
answer truly.

LEONATO:
I charge thee do so.

*(looking to DP)*

*(DP Xing to where Cl is, Cl
counters L)*

*(Leo takes Her's hand, brings
her DS 2 steps)*

CLAUDIO:
What man did you talk with last night
from out of your window between twelve
and one?

HERO:
I talked with no man at that hour, my
lord.

DON PEDRO:
Leonato, I am sorry you must hear this. On
my honor, myself, my brother, and this poor
distressed Count saw her, heard her, at
that time last night talk with a brute
out of her bedroom window, who has, like a
scoundrel, confessed to the thousand vile
encounters they have secretly had.

DON JOHN:
Pretty lady, I am sorry for your extreme
misconduct.

CLAUDIO:
Oh Hero! Fare you well, so foul and yet so
fair! Farewell.

LEONATO:
Is there no man here with a dagger for me?
*[Hero swoons]*

BEATRICE:
Oh, cousin! Why do you swoon?

DON JOHN:
Come, let's go. These matters, having come
to light, have smothered her spirits up.
*[exit Don Pedro, Don John & Claudio]*

BENEDICK:
How is the lady?

BEATRICE:
Dead, I think. Help, uncle! Hero! Why,
Hero! Uncle! Signior Benedick! Friar!

CLAUDIO:
What man was he talked with you yester-night out at your window betwixt twelve and one?

*(stepping DS to be level with Her)*

HERO:
I talked with no man at that hour, my lord.

DON PEDRO:
Leonato, I am sorry you must hear. Upon my honor, myself, my brother, and this grieved Count did see her, hear her, at that hour last night talk with a ruffian at her chamber window, who hath, like a villain, confessed the vile encounters they have had a thousand times in secret.

*(stepping DS between Her & Cl)*

DON JOHN:
Pretty lady, I am sorry for thy much misgovernment.

*(Xing DL of Cl)*

CLAUDIO:
O Hero! Fare thee well, most foul, most fair! Farewell.

*(Xing to Her, DP counters L)*

LEONATO:
Hath no man's dagger here a point for me?
*[Hero swoons]*

*(Her falls at Leo's feet, her head SR)*

BEATRICE:
Why, cousin! Wherefore sink you down?

*(rushing to SR of Her, kneeling to try to comfort her)*

DON JOHN:
Come, let us go. These things, come thus to light, smother her spirits up.
*[exit Don Pedro, Don John & Claudio]*

*(exit SL)*

BENEDICK:
How doth the lady?

*(Xing R 2 steps)*

BEATRICE:
Dead, I think. Help, uncle! Hero! Why, Hero! Uncle! Signior Benedick! Friar!

*(trying to revive Her)*

**Act Four · Scene 1**　　**vernacular**

LEONATO:
Death is the most appropriate shield to
hide her shame.

BEATRICE:
How are you, cousin Hero?

FRIAR FRANCIS:
Let me console you, lady.

LEONATO:
Do not live, Hero, do not open your eyes—
for if I thought you would not quickly
die, I would take your life myself. Oh,
why were you ever lovely to me? Why hadn't
I extended charity to a beggar's child at
my door, who, if she'd been besmirched
like this and dragged down in disgrace, I
could have said, 'I have no part in this;
this shame comes from unknown sources?'
But mine, and mine who I loved, and mine
who I praised, and mine who I was proud of.
Oh, she is fallen into a pit of ink, and
the wide seas have too few drops to wash
her clean again.

BENEDICK:
Sir, sir, be patient. As for me, I am
so amazed by this I don't know what to say.

BEATRICE:
Oh, on my soul my cousin is wrongfully
accused!

BENEDICK:
Lady, did you share her bedroom last night?

BEATRICE:
No, truly I did not—although until last
night, I have, for this past year, shared
her room.

LEONATO:
Confirmed, confirmed! Would the two
princes lie? Would Claudio lie, who loved
her so? Get away from her, let her die!

Act Four·Scene 1 **original abridged**

Act Four·Scene 1   **stage directions**

LEONATO:
Death is the fairest cover for her
shame that may be wished for.

BEATRICE:
How now, cousin Hero?

*(Her opens her eyes)*

FRIAR FRANCIS:
Have comfort, lady.

*(Xing to L of Leo)*

LEONATO:
Do not live, Hero, do not ope thine eyes—
for did I think thou would'st not quickly
die, myself would strike at thy life. O,
why ever wast thou lovely in my eyes?
Why had I not with a charitable hand took
up a beggar's issue at my gates, who
smirched thus, and mired with infamy, I
might have said, 'No part of it is mine;
this shame derives itself from unknown
loins'? But mine, and mine I loved, and
mine I praised, and mine that I was proud
on. O, she is fallen into a pit of ink,
that the wide sea hath drops too few to
wash her clean again.

BENEDICK:
Sir, sir, be patient. For my part I am
so attired in wonder, I know not what
to say.

BEATRICE:
O, on my soul my cousin is belied!

BENEDICK:
Lady, were you her bedfellow last

BEATRICE:
No, truly, not—although until night,
I have this twelvemonth been her
bedfellow.

LEONATO:
Confirmed, confirmed! Would the two
princes lie? And Claudio lie, who loved
her so? Hence from her, let her die!

FRIAR FRANCIS:
Listen to me a moment. I have been watching
the lady. Her eyes burn with a fire that
contradicts the allegations these princes
have made against her virginity. Call me
a fool—never trust my observations, my
age, my position, nor my teachings, if this
sweet lady does not lie here innocent of
these erroneous attacks. Lady, who is this
man you are accused of seeing?

HERO:
Those who accuse me know—I know none.
Oh my father, if you can prove that any man
conversed with me at inappropriate times,
or that I exchanged words with any creature
last night, then disown me, hate me, torture
me to death!

FRIAR FRANCIS:
There is some strange mistaking on the
princes' part.

BENEDICK:
Two of them are without doubt honorable, and if they've been misled in
this, it's been by John the bastard,
who only exists to stir up trouble.

LEONATO:
If they've spoken the truth about her, these
hands will tear her to pieces. If they've
lied about her, the proudest of them shall
pay for it.

FRIAR FRANCIS:
Take a minute, and let me advise you. The
princes have left your daughter here for
dead. Let her for now be secretly kept in,
and put it out that she is indeed dead.

LEONATO:
What will this do?

FRIAR FRANCIS:
Truly, if this is well executed, it shall

FRIAR FRANCIS:
Hear me a little. I have been noting
the lady. In her eye there hath appeared a
fire to burn the errors that these princes
hold against her maiden truth. Call me a
fool—trust not my observations, my age,
my reverence, nor divinity, if this sweet
lady lie not guiltless here under some
biting error. Lady, what man is he you
are accused of?

HERO:
They know that do accuse me—I know none.
O my father, prove you that any man
with me conversed at hours unmeet,
or that I yesternight maintained the
change of words with any creature,
refuse me, hate me, torture me to death!

FRIAR FRANCIS:
There is some strange misprision in the
princes.

BENEDICK:
Two of them have the very bent of honor,
and if their wisdoms be misled in this,
the practice of it lives in John the
bastard, whose spirits toil in frame
of villainies.

LEONATO:
If they speak truth of her, these hands
shall tear her. If they wrong her honor,
the proudest of them shall well hear of
it.

FRIAR FRANCIS:
Pause awhile, and let my counsel sway you.
Your daughter here the princes left for
dead. Let her awhile be secretly kept in,
and publish it that she is dead indeed.

LEONATO:
What will this do?

FRIAR FRANCIS:
Marry, this well carried, shall on her

*(X DS a bit & kneeling to Her)*

*(rise, X DSL of Ben)*

*(Xing to R of FF, Ben counters R)*

on her behalf turn these slanders
into remorse. Her dying, as we must
maintain, at the very moment that she
was accused, shall be lamented, pitied,
and excused by everyone who hears of it—
for it turns out that we never treasure
what we have while we possess it, but
having lost it, we discover the value we
never noticed while it was ours. So it
will be with Claudio. When he hears that
she died as a result of his words, then
he shall mourn and wish he had not accused
her—no, even if he believed the accusation
to be true. And have no doubt but that
the result of this will be even better than
I could conjecture.

BENEDICK:
Signior Leonato, take the friar's advice.
And even though, as you know, I am very
close to the Prince and Claudio, I shall,
on my honor, deal with this secretly and
justly.

LEONATO:
Since I am overwhelmed with grief, I must
hold on to even the smallest ray of hope.

FRIAR FRANCIS:
Well done, Let us go, Come lady, die so
you might live. *[all exit except Beatrice
& Benedick]*

BENEDICK:
Lady Beatrice, have you wept all this
while?

BEATRICE:
Yes, and I will weep a while longer.

BENEDICK:
I would not like that.

BEATRICE:
You've no reason to, I do it of my own free
will.

behalf, change slander to remorse. She
dying, as it must be maintained upon the
instant that she was accused, shall be
lamented, pitied, and excused of every
hearer—for so it falls out that what
we have we prize not whiles we enjoy it,
but being lost, why then we find the
virtue that possession would not show
us whiles it was ours. So will it fare
with Claudio. When he shall hear she
died upon his words, then shall he mourn
and wish he had not so accused her—no,
though he thought the accusation true.
And doubt not but success will fashion the
event in better shape than I can lay it
down in likelihood.

BENEDICK:
Signior Leonato, let the friar advise
you—and though you know my love is very
much unto the Prince and Claudio, yet, by
mine honor, I will deal with this secretly
and justly.

*(X DS to R of Leo)*

LEONATO:
Being that I flow in grief, the smallest
twine may lead me.

FRIAR FRANCIS:
Well consented. Presently away. Come
lady, die to live. *[all exit except
Beatrice & Benedick]*

*(FF & Ben help Her up & bring
her UC, Leo & Ant follow, as
Bea X to DR bench, sit weeping
quietly, all exit UC except
Ben who turns, sees Bea, speaks
softly to her from UC)*

BENEDICK:
Lady Beatrice, have you wept all this
while?

BEATRICE:
Yea, and I will weep a while longer.

BENEDICK:
I will not desire that.

BEATRICE:
You have no reason, I do it freely.

BENEDICK:
I certainly believe your fair cousin has
been wronged.

BEATRICE:
Ah, what I might owe to the man who would
right her honor.

BENEDICK:
Is there any way to show such friendship?

BEATRICE:
A very easy way, but I haven't such a friend.

BENEDICK:
I do love nothing in the world so well as
you—isn't that strange?

BEATRICE:
As strange as—the thing I know not. It
were as possible for me to say I loved nothing
so well as you—but believe me not—and
yet I lie not—I confess nothing, nor I
deny nothing. I am sorry for my cousin.


BENEDICK:
By my sword, Beatrice, you love me.

BEATRICE:
Do not swear and then eat your words.

BENEDICK:
I will swear by it that you love me, and
I'll make him eat my sword who says I don't
love you.

BEATRICE:
Will you not eat your words?

BENEDICK:
With no sauce that can be devised. I
swear I love you.

BEATRICE:
Why then, God forgive me!

| Act Four·Scene 1 **original abridged** | Act Four·Scene 1   **stage directions** |
| --- | --- |

BENEDICK:
Surely I do believe your fair cousin is
wronged.

*(Xing to RC)*

BEATRICE:
Ah, how much might the man deserve of me
that would right her.

BENEDICK:
Is there any way to show such friendship?

BEATRICE:
A very even way, but no such friend.

BENEDICK:
I do love nothing in the world so well
as you—is not that strange?

*(Xing & kneeling UL of Bea)*

BEATRICE:
As strange as—the thing I know not. It
were as possible for me to say I loved
nothing so well as you—but believe
me not—and yet I lie not—I confess
nothing, nor I deny nothing. I am sorry
for my cousin.

BENEDICK:
By my sword, Beatrice, thou lovest me.

BEATRICE:
Do not swear and eat it.

BENEDICK:
I will swear by it that you love me, and
I will make him eat it that says I love
not you.

BEATRICE:
Will you not eat your words?

BENEDICK:
With no sauce that can be devised. I
protest I love thee.

BEATRICE:
Why then, God forgive me!

**Act Four · Scene 1          vernacular**

BENEDICK:
For what offence, sweet Beatrice?

BEATRICE:
You have caught me at the perfect moment,
I was about to protest that I loved you.

BENEDICK:
Then do it with all your heart.

BEATRICE:
I love you with so much of my heart that
none is left to protest.

BENEDICK:
Come on, command me to do anything for you.

BEATRICE:
Kill Claudio!

BENEDICK:
Ha! Not for the wide world!

BEATRICE:
You kill me to deny it. Farewell.

BENEDICK:
Stay, sweet Beatrice.

BEATRICE:
I am gone, though I am here. There
is no love in you. No, I beg you let me go.

BENEDICK:
Beatrice–

BEATRICE:
Truly, I will go.

BENEDICK:
We'll be friends first.

BEATRICE:
You dare to think that you can be my friend
and not share my enemies.

| Act Four • Scene 1 **original abridged** | Act Four • Scene 1    **stage directions** |
| --- | --- |

**BENEDICK:**
What offence, sweet Beatrice?

**BEATRICE:**
You have stayed me in a happy hour, I
was about to protest I loved you.

**BENEDICK:**
And do it with all thy heart.

**BEATRICE:**
I love you with so much of my heart that
none is left to protest.

**BENEDICK:**
Come, bid me do anything for thee.

**BEATRICE:**
Kill Claudio!

**BENEDICK:**
Ha! Not for the wide world!          *(rise, Xing L)*

**BEATRICE:**
You kill me to deny it. Farewell.          *(rise, Xing US)*

**BENEDICK:**
Tarry, sweet Beatrice.          *(Ben intercepts her RC, holds*
                                                  *her arms)*

**BEATRICE:**
I am gone, though I am here. There is
no love in you. Nay, I pray you let me go.          *(trying to break free)*

**BENEDICK:**
Beatrice–          *(still holding her)*

**BEATRICE:**
In faith, I will go.          *(breaking free)*

**BENEDICK:**
We'll be friends first.

**BEATRICE:**
You dare easier be friends with me than          *(face to face with Ben)*
fight with mine enemy.

BENEDICK:
Is Claudio your enemy?

BEATRICE:
Isn't he proven an absolute villain,
who has slandered, scorned, dishonored
my cousin? Oh if only I were
a man! What, take her hand until
they come to join hands, and then with
public accusations, bare-faced slander,
unmitigated rancor—Oh God if only I were
a man! I would eat his heart in the
marketplace.

BENEDICK:
Hear me, Beatrice—

BEATRICE:
Talk with a man out of a window! A charming
thing to say!

BENEDICK:
No, but Beatrice—

BEATRICE:
Sweet Hero! She is wronged, she is
slandered, she is ruined.

BENEDICK:
Beat—

BEATRICE:
Princes and counts! A fine count! Oh if only
I were a man for his sake, or if I had any
friend who would be a man for my sake! But
manhood is dissolved into mincing manners,
valor into flattery, and men are 'all talk.'
A man is as valiant as Hercules if he tells
a lie and swears to it. I cannot be a man
with wishing, therefore I will die a woman
with grieving.

BENEDICK:
Wait, good Beatrice, I swear by this hand,
I love you.

BENEDICK:
Is Claudio thine enemy?

BEATRICE:
Is 'a not approved in the height a
villain, that hath slandered, scorned,
dishonored my kinswoman? O that I were
a man! What, bear her in hand until
they come to take hands, and then with
public accusation, uncovered slander,
unmitigated rancor–O God that I were
a man! I would eat his heart in the
marketplace.

BENEDICK:
Hear me, Beatrice–

BEATRICE:
Talk with a man out at a window! A proper
saying!

BENEDICK:
Nay, but Beatrice–

BEATRICE:
Sweet Hero! She is wronged, she is
slandered, she is undone.

BENEDICK:
Beat–

BEATRICE:
Princes and counties! A goodly count! O
that I were a man for his sake, or that
I had any friend would be a man for my
sake! But manhood is melted into curtsies,
valor into compliment, and men are turned
into tongue. He is now as valiant as
Hercules that tells a lie and swears it.
I cannot be a man with wishing, therefore
I will die a woman with grieving.

BENEDICK:
Tarry, good Beatrice, by this hand I
love thee.

(Xing DL)

(Xing to her)

(turning to him)

(Xing SR, DS of Ben)

(during this speech, Bea paces
back & forth DS of Ben)

(Bea starts UC)

(Ben grabs her hand & kneels
down to her)

---

## Act Four·Scene 1 — vernacular

**BEATRICE:**
Use it for my love some other way than swearing by it.

**BENEDICK:**
Do you think in your soul that Count Claudio has wronged Hero?

**BEATRICE:**
Yes, as surely as I have a thought or a soul.

**BENEDICK:**
Enough! I am committed, I will challenge him. I will kiss your hand, and I will leave you. On my honor, Claudio shall pay for this. Go comfort your cousin. I must say she is dead—and so farewell.
*[they exit]*

---

## Act Four·Scene 2 — scene analysis

In this scene, we have Dogberry and Verges carrying out Leonato's orders to interrogate Borachio and Conrade. They have gotten the Sexton from the church to assist them because he can write.

Dogberry's questioning goes nowhere. The Sexton finally tells him that he must call forth the Watch to make their accusation against the prisoners.

The Sexton is able to corroborate the testimony that the Watch gives. He then tells Dogberry to bring the bound prisoners to Leonato's and says that he will go ahead and show him the report.

*Dogberry Dictionary*

| | |
|---|---|
| dissembly | assembly |
| eftest | deftest or aptest |
| perjury | slander |
| suspect | respect |

---

## Act Four·Scene 2 — vernacular

*[enter Dogberry, Verges, Sexton & the Watch with Conrade & Borachio]*
**DOGBERRY:**
Has our whole <u>dissembly</u> appeared?

**VERGES:**
No, that's right.

**SEXTON:**
Which are the offenders that are to be examined? Let them come and face Master Constable.

**DOGBERRY:**
Yes indeed, let them come and face me. What is your name, friend?

**BORACHIO:**
Borachio.

## Act Four · Scene 1  original abridged

BEATRICE:
Use it for my love some other way than
swearing by it.

BENEDICK:
Think you in your soul the Count Claudio
hath wronged Hero?

BEATRICE:
Yea, as sure as I have a thought or a
soul.

BENEDICK:
Enough! I am engaged, I will challenge
him. I will kiss your hand, and so I leave
you. By this hand, Claudio shall render me
a dear account. Go comfort your cousin.
I must say she is dead—and so farewell.
[they exit]

## Act Four · Scene 1  stage directions

(rises)
(kisses her hand)
(holding up his right hand)

(Ben exits SL, Bea looks off
after him for a beat, exits
UC)

## Act Four · Scene 2  original abridged

[enter Dogberry, Verges, Sexton, & the
Watch with Conrade & Borachio]
DOGBERRY:
Is our whole dissembly appeared?

VERGES:
Nay, that's certain.

SEXTON:
Which are the offenders that are to be
examined? Let them come before Master
Constable.

DOGBERRY:
Yea, marry, let them come before me. What
is your name, friend?

BORACHIO:
Borachio.

## Act Four · Scene 2  stage directions

(Dog & Ver enter DL, Watch follow
prodding Con & Bor on, all
cluster C)

(enters DL, has pencil & pad,
X to UR bench, sit, Dog X to
R of Sext, Ver X DL of bench,
Con & Bor stand on angle R
of C facing DL, Bor R of Con,
Watch stand behind them)
(Dog X to Bor)

**Act Four · Scene 2**                    **vernacular**

DOGBERRY: *[to Sexton]*
Please write down 'Borachio.' *[to Conrade]*
Yours, sonny?

CONRADE:
I am a gentleman, sir, and my name is
Conrade.

DOGBERRY: *[to Sexton]*
Write down 'Master Gentleman Conrade.' *[to
Conrade & Borachio]* Masters, are you God-
fearing men?

CONRADE & BORACHIO:
Yes, sir, we hope.

DOGBERRY: *[to Sexton]*
Write down that they hope they are God-
fearing men. *[to Conrade & Borachio]*
Masters, it is proved that you are no
more than lying rascals. What do you say
for yourselves?

CONRADE:
Truly, sir, we say we are not.

DOGBERRY: *[to Verges]*
A smart-mouthed fellow. *[to Borachio]*
I say to you, it is thought that you are
lying rascals.

BORACHIO:
Sir, I say to you we are not.

DOGBERRY: *[to Verges]*
I swear to God, they're in cahoots. *[to
Sexton]* Have you writ down that they are
not?

SEXTON:
Master Constable, you're going about this
examination all wrong. You must call forth
The Watch who have accused them.

DOGBERRY:
Yes, indeed, that's the <u>eftest</u> way. Let the

| Act Four·Scene 2 **original abridged** | Act Four·Scene 2  **stage directions** |
|---|---|
| DOGBERRY: *[to Sexton]*<br>Pray write down 'Borachio.' *[to Conrade]*<br>Yours, sirrah? | *(Xing to Sext, then to Con)* |
| CONRADE:<br>I am a gentleman, sir, and my name is<br>Conrade. | |
| DOGBERRY: *[to Sexton]*<br>Write down 'Master Gentleman Conrade.' *[to Conrade & Borachio]* Masters, do you serve God? | *(Xing to Sext, then back to Con & Bor)* |
| CONRADE & BORACHIO:<br>Yea, sir, we hope. | |
| DOGBERRY: *[to Sexton]*<br>Write down that they hope they serve God.<br>*[to Conrade & Borachio]* Masters, it is<br>proved that you are little better than<br>false knaves. How answer you for your-<br>selves? | *(Xing to Sext then back to Con & Bor)* |
| CONRADE:<br>Marry, sir, we say we are none. | |
| DOGBERRY: [to Verges]<br>A marvelous witty fellow. *[to Borachio]*<br>I say to you, it is thought you are<br>false knaves. | *(looking to Ver)*<br>*(Xing to Bor)* |
| BORACHIO:<br>Sir, I say to you we are none. | |
| DOGBERRY: *[to Verges]*<br>Fore God, they are both in a tale. *[to<br>Sexton]* Have you writ down that they are<br>none? | *(looking to Ver)*<br>*(Xing to Sext)* |
| SEXTON:<br>Master Constable, you go not the way to<br>examine. You must call forth The Watch<br>that are their accusers. | |
| DOGBERRY:<br>Yea, marry, that's the <u>eftest</u> way. Let the | |

watch step forward. *[to Watch]* I order you in the Prince's name—accuse these men.

FIRST WATCH:
This man said, sir, that Don John, the Prince's brother, was a villain.

DOGBERRY: *[to Sexton]*
Write down 'Prince John a villain.' *[to Verges]* Why this is downright <u>perjury</u> to call a prince's brother villain.

SEXTON:
What else did you hear him say?

SECOND WATCH:
Truly, that he had received a thousand gold coins from Don John for wrongfully accusing the Lady Hero.

DOGBERRY:
Downright burglary!

VERGES:
Yes, that's it.

SEXTON:
What else, fellow?

FIRST WATCH:
That Count Claudio meant to disgrace Hero in front of the whole assembly and not to marry her.

DOGBERRY:
Oh villain!

SEXTON:
What else?

SECOND WATCH:
That's all.

SEXTON:
And, masters, that is more than you can deny. Prince John secretly snuck off this

watch come forth. *[to Watch]* I charge you in the Prince's name accuse these men.

FIRST WATCH:
This man said, sir, that Don John, the Prince's brother, was a villain.

DOGBERRY: *[to Sexton]*
Write down 'Prince John a villain.' *[to Verges]* Why this is flat <u>perjury</u> to call a prince's brother villain.

SEXTON:
What heard you him say else?

SECOND WATCH:
Marry, that he had received a thousand ducats of Don John for accusing the Lady Hero wrongfully.

DOGBERRY:
Flat burglary!

VERGES:
Yea, that it is.

SEXTON:
What else, fellow?

FIRST WATCH:
That Count Claudio did mean to disgrace Hero before the whole assembly and not marry her.

DOGBERRY:
O villain!

SEXTON:
What else?

SECOND WATCH:
This is all.

SEXTON:
And this is more, masters, than you can deny. Prince John is this morning secretly

*(Watch step to sides of Bor & Con)*

*(pointing to Bor)*

*(rise, X DL of Con, W2 counter L)*

morning. Hero was just this way accused, and as a result of the grief over this, suddenly died. Master Constable, let these men be bound and be brought to Leonato's. I will go ahead and show him their examination. *[exit]*

DOGBERRY: *[to Watch]*
Come on, bind them. [to Borachio] You naughty boy!

CONRADE: *[to Dogberry]*
Get lost! you're an ass, you are an ass!

DOGBERRY:
Do you not <u>suspect</u> my position? Do you not <u>suspect</u> my age? Oh that he were here to write down I'm an ass! But, masters, remember that I am an ass—though it's not written down. I am a wise fellow; and what's more, an officer; and what's more, head of a household; and what's more, as good-looking a hunk as any in Messina! *[to Watch]* Bring him away. Oh that I had been writ down an ass! *[all exit]*

Leonato, now convinced in his soul that Hero is innocent, wishes revenge. His brother Antonio tries to calm him.

Don Pedro and Claudio appear, and Leonato tries to challenge Claudio to a duel, but Claudio refuses to deal with him. When Don Pedro won't respond to Leonato's plea, Leonato and Antonio depart.

Benedick enters intending to fulfill his promise to Beatrice. Don Pedro and Claudio think Benedick is jesting when he makes his challenge. Benedick leaves them, and they begin to realize that Benedick is in earnest.

Dogberry enters along with the Watch, who have Borachio and Conrade in tow. Don Pedro asks why his brother's men are under arrest. Dogberry's

*[enter Leonato & Antonio]*
ANTONIO:
If you go on like this, you'll kill yourself.

LEONATO:
Do not advise me, nor let anyone try to comfort me except one who has been wronged as I have. Show me a father who so loved his child, whose joy of her was as great as mine, and ask him to talk of patience. Men can counsel and try to comfort a grief which they haven't suffered, but having felt it, that counsel turns into passion. There has never yet been a philosopher who could stand a toothache with patience.

## Act Four · Scene 2   original abridged

stolen away. Hero was in this manner accused, and upon the grief of this suddenly died. Master Constable, let these men be bound and be brought to Leonato's. I will go before and show him their examination. *[exit]*

DOGBERRY: *[to Watch]*
Come, bind them. [to Borachio]
Thou naughty varlet!

CONRADE: *[to Dogberry]*
Away! you are an ass, you are an ass!

DOGBERRY:
Dost thou not <u>suspect</u> my place? Dost thou not <u>suspect</u> my years? O that he were here to write me down an ass! But, masters, remember that I am an ass—though it be not written down. I am a wise fellow; and which is more, an officer; and which is more, a householder; and which is more, as pretty a piece of flesh as any in Messina! *[to Watch]* Bring him away. O that I had been writ down as ass! *[all exit]*

## Act Five · Scene 1   original abridged

*[enter Leonato & Antonio]*
ANTONIO:
If you go on thus, you will kill yourself.

LEONATO:
Give not me counsel, nor let no comforter delight mine ear but such a one whose wrongs do suit with mine. Bring me a father that so loved his child, whose joy of her so overwhelmed like mine, and bid him speak of patience. Men can counsel and speak comfort to that grief which they themselves not feel; but tasting it, their counsel turns to passion. There was never yet philosopher that could endure the toothache patiently.

## Act Four · Scene 2   stage directions

*(turning to Dog)*

*(exits DL)*

*(Watch take rope from their pockets, X behind Con & Bor to bind their hands)*

*(Dog steps back, amazed)*

*(Watch take Bor & Con off DL, Dog & Ver following)*

## Act Five · Scene 1   stage directions

*(Leo enters UC, looking for Cl, Xing SR, Ant follows Xing to RC)*

*(turning to Ant)*

*(Xing SL, looking around, Ant follows, Xing to C)*

*Cont.*
answer is so confusing that Don Pedro must ask the arrested men directly, and Borachio tells him of his part in the plot to destroy Hero's reputation.

At this moment Leonato, who has been told of this news, comes out to see the villainous Borachio and to again accuse Don Pedro and Claudio of complicity in the death of Hero. They now accept responsibility and offer to atone for their actions.

Leonato puts two stipulations on his forgiveness: that Don Pedro and Claudio inform the populace of Messina of Hero's innocence and that Claudio agree to marry the "daughter" of Antonio.

Leonato suggests that Margaret had a hand in the deception. Borachio defends her by saying that she was ignorant of any wrongdoing. Leonato thanks Dogberry for his "care and honest pains," and all depart.

### Dogberry Dictionary

| | |
|---|---|
| slanders | slanderers |
| reformed | informed |
| plaintiffs | defendants |
| God save the foundation! | (untranslatable) |

*Note: "God save the foundation" is what professional beggars would say when they received a hand-out—not quite appropriate for the moment, but Dogberry is trying!*

ANTONIO:
Yet don't take all this pain onto yourself. Make those who have wronged you suffer too.

LEONATO:
There you make sense, I will do that. My very soul tells me that Hero has been falsely accused; and Claudio shall learn that; so shall the Prince and all the others who dishonored her. *[enter Don Pedro & Claudio]*

ANTONIO:
Here comes the Prince and Claudio.

DON PEDRO:
Good evening.

CLAUDIO:
Good day to you.

LEONATO:
Listen, my lords—

DON PEDRO:
We are in a hurry, Leonato.

LEONATO:
In a hurry, my lord! Are you in such a hurry now? Well, no matter.

DON PEDRO:
Oh, don't quarrel with us, good old man.

LEONATO:
By God, you wrong me, you hypocrite, you! Know Claudio, to your face, that you have so harmed my innocent child and me, that I am forced to ignore the privileges of my age and challenge you to a duel. I say you have lied about my innocent child; your slanders have gone through and through her heart, and she now lies buried with her ancestors in a tomb where scandal never dwelt, except for this, caused by your villainy!

ANTONIO:
Yet bend not all the harm upon yourself.
Make those that do offend you suffer too.

*(X to UL bench, sit UR end)*

LEONATO:
There thou speaks't reason, I will do so.
My soul doth tell me Hero is belied; and
that shall Claudio know; so shall the
Prince and all of them that thus dishonor
her. *[enter Don Pedro and Claudio]*

*(Xing to Ant, sit DL of Ant
on bench)*

*(Cl & DP enter DR, walking L,
see Leo & Ant, stop DRC)*

ANTONIO:
Here comes the Prince and Claudio.

*(Ant & Leo rise)*

DON PEDRO:
Good den.

CLAUDIO:
Good day to you.

LEONATO:
Hear you, my lords—

*(Xing DC to intercept them)*

DON PEDRO:
We have some haste, Leonato.

LEONATO:
Some haste, my lord! Are you so hasty
now? Well, all is one.

DON PEDRO:
Nay, do not quarrel with us, good old
man.

LEONATO:
Marry, thou dost wrong me, thou dissem-
bler, thou! Know, Claudio, to thy head,
thou hast so wronged mine innocent child
and me that I am forced to lay my reverence by and do challenge thee. I say thou
hast belied mine innocent child; thy
slander hath gone through and through
her heart, and she lies buried with her
ancestors in a tomb where never scandal
slept, save this of hers, framed by thy
villainy!

## Act Five • Scene 1                    vernacular

CLAUDIO:
My villainy?

LEONATO:
Yours, Claudio—yours I say.

DON PEDRO:
You say wrong, old man.

LEONATO:
My lord, I'll prove it if he dares, despite
his fencing skills, his being in practice
and his youth.

CLAUDIO:
Go away! I will not deal with you.

LEONATO:
You think you can dismiss me? You have
killed my child. If you kill me, boy, you
will kill a man.

ANTONIO:
He shall kill two of us. Come follow me,
boy—come, sir boy, come follow me.

LEONATO:
Brother—

ANTONIO:
God knows I loved my niece, and she is dead
slandered to death by villains—boys, apes
bigshots, silly boys, sissies.

LEONATO:
Brother Antony—

DON PEDRO:
Gentlemen both, we will not try your
patience any longer. My heart is sorry for
your daughter's death; but on my honor
she was accused of nothing but what was
true and proven so.

LEONATO:
My lord—

CLAUDIO:
My villainy?

LEONATO:
Thine, Claudio—thine I say.

DON PEDRO:
You say not right, old man.

LEONATO:
My lord, I'll prove it if he dare, despite his nice fence, his practice and his youth.

CLAUDIO:
Away! I will not have to do with you.

LEONATO:
Canst thou so daff me? Thou hast killed my child. If thou killst me, boy, thou shalt kill a man.

ANTONIO:
He shall kill two of us. Come, follow me, boy. Come, sir boy, come follow me.

LEONATO:
Brother—

ANTONIO:
God knows I loved my niece, and she is dead, slandered to death by villains. Boys, apes, braggarts, Jacks, milksops!

LEONATO:
Brother Anthony—

DON PEDRO:
Gentlemen both, we will not wake your patience. My heart is sorry for your daughter's death; but on my honor she was charged with nothing but what was true and very full of proof.

LEONATO:
My lord—

*(Xing to between Leo & Cl, putting up his fists)*

*(trying to restrain Ant)*

*(shadow-boxing around threateningly at Cl & DP)*

*(still trying to restrain Ant)*

## Act Five • Scene 1    vernacular

DON PEDRO:
I will not listen to you.

LEONATO:
No? Come, brother, away! I will be heard!
*[Leonato and Antonio exit]*

*[enter Benedick]*
DON PEDRO:
See, see! Here comes the man we went
to seek.

CLAUDIO:
Now, signior, what's new?

BENEDICK:
Good day, my lord.

CLAUDIO:
We've been all over looking for you, we
are potently depressed and would gladly
have it driven away. Will you use your
wit on us?

BENEDICK:
It is in my scabbard; shall I draw it?

DON PEDRO:
Do you wear your wit in your sword belt?
*[to Claudio]* As I'm an honest man, he looks
pale. *[back to Benedick]* Are you sick or
angry?

BENEDICK: *[to Claudio]*
Shall I whisper a word in your ear?

CLAUDIO:
God save me—a challenge!

BENEDICK:
You are a villain. I'm not joking; I
will prove it however you dare, with
whatever you dare and when you dare.
Do right by this or I'll proclaim you
a coward. You have killed a sweet lady
and her death shall hang heavy on you.
Let me hear from you.

Act Five·Scene 1  **original abridged**

DON PEDRO:
I will not hear you.

LEONATO:
No? Come, brother, away! I will be heard!
*[Leonato & Antonio exit]*

*[enter Benedick]*
DON PEDRO:
See, see! Here comes the man we went
to seek.

CLAUDIO:
Now, signior, what news?

BENEDICK:
Good day, my lord.

CLAUDIO:
We have been up and down to seek thee,
for we are high-proof melancholy and
would fain have it beaten away. Wilt
thou use thy wit?

BENEDICK:
It is in my scabbard; shall I draw it?

DON PEDRO:
Dost thou wear thy wit by thy side?
*[to Claudio]* As I am an honest man, he looks
pale. *[back to Benedick]* Art thou sick, or
angry?

BENEDICK: *[to Claudio]*
Shall I speak a word in your ear?

CLAUDIO:
God bless me from a challenge!

BENEDICK:
You are a villain. I jest not; I will
make it good how you dare, with what
you dare and when you dare. Do me right
or I will protest your cowardice. You
have killed a sweet lady and her death
shall fall heavy on you. Let me hear
from you.

Act Five·Scene 1  **stage directions**

*(Xing past Cl to Ant & Leo, Cl counters R)*

*(pulling Ant UC & off, with appropriate ad libs from Ant & Leo)*
*(enter SL with sword, X LC)*

*(DP & Cl X to meet him)*

*(touching hilt of sword)*

*(stepping DS & facing Cl)*

*(Xing past DP to Cl, DP counters L)*

Act Five · Scene 1                    **vernacular**

CLAUDIO:
Well, I'll meet you so that I may have a
good time.

BENEDICK:
Take care, boy, you understand me. *[to
Don Pedro]* My lord, for the many kind-
nesses you have shown me, I thank you.
I must discontinue your company. Your
brother the bastard has fled from Messina.
You have among yourselves killed a sweet
and innocent lady. *[he exits]*

DON PEDRO:
He is serious.

CLAUDIO:
Completely serious.

DON PEDRO:
And he has challenged you.

CLAUDIO:
Very sincerely.

DON PEDRO:
But, wait. Didn't he say my brother had
fled?

*[enter Dogberry, Borachio, Conrade & the
Watch]*
DOGBERRY:
Come on, sir, you must be dealt with.

DON PEDRO:
What's this? My brother's men under arrest?

CLAUDIO:
Ask what their offence is, my lord.

DON PEDRO:
Officer what crime have these men
committed?

DOGBERRY:
Indeed, sir, they have spoken untruths,

| Act Five · Scene 1  **original abridged** | Act Five · Scene 1  **stage directions** |
|---|---|

CLAUDIO:
Well, I will meet you, so I may have
good cheer.

BENEDICK:
Fare you well, boy, you know my mind.
*[to Don Pedro]* My lord, for your many          *(turning to DP)*
courtesies I thank you. I must discon-
tinue your company. Your brother the
bastard is fled from Messina. You have
among you killed a sweet and innocent
lady. *[he exits]*          *(exit UC)*

DON PEDRO:
He is in earnest.

CLAUDIO:
In most profound earnest.

DON PEDRO:
And hath challenged thee.

CLAUDIO:
Most sincerely.

DON PEDRO:
But, soft. Did he not say my brother
was fled?

*[enter Dogberry, Borachio, Conrade & the*          *(Dog prods Con & Bor on from*
*Watch]*          *DL, seeing DP, they stop DL,*
DOGBERRY:          *Watch follow stopping at DL*
Come you, sir, you must be looked to.          *edge of stage)*

DON PEDRO:
How now? My brother's men bound?

CLAUDIO:
Hearken after their offence, my lord.

DON PEDRO:
Officer, what offence have these men          *(Xing DS a bit)*
done?

DOGBERRY:
Marry, sir, they have spoken untruths,

secondarily they are <u>slanders</u>, sixth and
lastly they have lied about a lady, thirdly
they have verified unjust things, and to
conclude, they are lying knaves.

DON PEDRO:
First I ask you what they have done,
thirdly I ask you what is their offence,
sixth and lastly why they are under
arrest, and to conclude, what they are
accused of.

CLAUDIO:
Cleverly done, and with his own mistakes.

DON PEDRO: *[to Borachio & Conrade]*
Who have you wronged, young sirs, that you
are handcuffed? This learned constable is
too crafty to be understood. What's your
offence?

BORACHIO:
Sweet Prince, listen, and let this Count
kill me. I have deceived your very own eyes.
What you wise gentlemen could not uncover,
these silly fools have brought to light,
who last night overheard me confessing
to this man, how Don John your brother
spurred me on to discredit the Lady Hero, how
you were brought into the orchard and saw
me woo Margaret dressed in Hero's clothes,
how you disgraced her when you should have
married her. The lady is dead because of my
own and my master's false accusations.

DON PEDRO:
Don't these words run through your blood
like a sword?

CLAUDIO:
I feel as though I'd drunk poison while he
spoke them. Sweet Hero, now I see you as
the precious vision that I first loved.

DOGBERRY:
By now the Sexton has <u>reformed</u> Signior

secondarily they are <u>slanders</u>, sixth
and lastly they have belied a lady,
thirdly they have verified unjust things,
and to conclude, they are lying knaves.

DON PEDRO:
First I ask thee what they have done,
thirdly I ask thee what's their offence,
sixth and lastly why they are committed,
and to conclude, what you lay to their
charge.

CLAUDIO:
Rightly reasoned, and in his own division.

DON PEDRO: *[to Borachio & Conrade]*
Who have you offended, masters, that you
are thus bound? This learned constable
is too cunning to be understood. What's
your offence?

BORACHIO:
Sweet Prince, hear me, and let this Count
kill me. I have deceived even your very
eyes. What your wisdoms could not discover,
these shallow fools have brought to light,
who in the night overheard me confessing
to this man, how Don John your brother
incensed me to slander the Lady Hero, how
you were brought into the orchard and saw
me court Margaret in Hero's garments, how
you disgraced her when you should marry
her. The lady is dead upon mine and my
master's false accusation.

DON PEDRO:
Runs not this speech like iron through
your blood?

CLAUDIO:
I have drunk poison whiles he uttered it.
Sweet Hero, now thy image doth appear in
the rare semblance that I loved it first.

DOGBERRY:
By this time our Sexton hath <u>reformed</u>

*(steps to DP & kneels)*

*(indicating Watch)*

*(indicating Con)*

*(turning to Cl)*

*(Cl Xing DRC, DP following to comfort Cl)*

*(directing this to DP)*

Leonato of the matter. Come, away
plaintiffs.

*[enter Leonato, Antonio & Sexton]*
LEONATO:
Which is the villain? Let me look in his
eyes so when I see another man like him I
may avoid him.

BORACHIO:
If you wish to know who wronged you, look
upon me.

LEONATO:
You have killed my innocent child.

BORACHIO:
Yes, I myself.

LEONATO:
No, not true, villain. Here are a pair
of honorable men—a third has fled—
who had a hand in my daughter's death.
*[sarcastically]* Record it with your great
and worthy deeds—it was bravely done.

CLAUDIO:
I don't know how to ask for your forgiveness. Yet I must speak. Choose your
revenge, impose on me whatever penance
you can devise for my sin; yet my only
sin was in mistaking.

DON PEDRO:
By my soul, mine too. To satisfy this good
old man, I will submit to any penance he'll
oblige me to.

LEONATO:
I cannot make you make my daughter live—
that is impossible—but I implore you
both to inform the people of Messina of her
innocence. Tomorrow morning come to my
house and since you could not
be my son-in-law, you can be my nephew. My
brother has a daughter who is almost identical

Signior Leonato of the matter. Come, away plaintiffs.

*[enter Leonato, Antonio & the Sexton]*
LEONATO:
Which is the villain? Let me see his eyes that when I note another man like him I may avoid him.

BORACHIO:
If you would know your wronger, look on me.

LEONATO:
Thou hast killed mine innocent child.

BORACHIO:
Yea, even I alone.

LEONATO:
No, not so, villain. Here stand a pair of honorable men—a third is fled— that had a hand in my daughter's death. *[sarcastically]* Record it with your high and worthy deeds—'twas bravely done.

CLAUDIO:
I know not how to pray your patience. Yet I must speak. Choose your revenge, impose me to what penance your invention can lay upon my sin; yet sinned I not but in mistaking.

DON PEDRO:
By my soul, nor I. Yet, to satisfy this good old man, I would bend under any heavy weight that he'll enjoin me to.

LEONATO:
I cannot bid you bid my daughter live— that were impossible—but I pray you both, possess the people in Messina how innocent she died. Tomorrow morning come you to my house, and since you could not be my son-in-law, be yet my nephew. My brother hath a daughter, almost the copy

*(starting towards C with Con & Bor)*

*(Leo enter UC, X C, Ant & Sext remain UC)*

*(taking a step to Leo)*

*(X DS to Bor)*

*(indicating DP & Cl)*

*(Xing to DR of Leo, kneels to Leo)*

*(Xing to DR of Cl, kneels to Leo)*

to my child who's dead. Give her the
title of wife that you should have given to her
cousin and that will satisfy my revenge.

CLAUDIO:
Oh noble sir, your kindness brings tears
to my eyes! I accept your offer.

LEONATO:
Tomorrow then I will expect you to come.
This wicked man shall be brought face to
face with Margaret, who I believe was
an accomplice in all this wrongdoing.

BORACHIO:
No, on my soul she was not, nor did she know
what she was doing when she spoke to me,
but has always been just and virtuous.

DOGBERRY:
Moreover, sir, this <u>plaintiff</u> here called
me ass. I beg you to take that into account
in his punishment.

LEONATO: *[to Dogberry]*
I thank you for your care and honest
efforts.

DOGBERRY:
Your honor speaks like a most thankful
and reverent youth, and I praise God
for you.

LEONATO:
There's something for your trouble.

DOGBERRY:
<u>God save the foundation</u>!

LEONATO:
Go, I relieve you of your prisoners and
I thank you.

DOGBERRY:
I leave an arch villain with your worship.
God keep your worship, I wish your worship

of my child that's dead. Give her the
right you should have given her cousin,
and so dies my revenge.

CLAUDIO:
O noble sir, your kindness doth wring
tears from me! I do embrace your offer.

LEONATO:
Tomorrow then I will expect your coming.
This naughty man shall face to face be
brought to Margaret, who I believe was
packed in all this wrong.

BORACHIO:
No, by my soul she was not, nor knew
not what she did when she spoke to me,
but always hath been just and virtuous.

DOGBERRY:
Moreover, sir, this <u>plaintiff</u> here, did
call me ass. I beseech you let it be
remembered in his punishment.

LEONATO: *[to Dogberry]*
I thank thee for thy care and honest
pains.

DOGBERRY:
Your worship speaks like a most thankful
and reverent youth, and I praise God
for you.

LEONATO:
There's for thy pains.

DOGBERRY:
<u>God save the foundation</u>!

LEONATO:
Go, I discharge thee of thy prisoner and
I thank thee.

DOGBERRY:
I leave an arrant knave with your worship.
God keep your worship! I wish your worship

*(DP & Cl rise)*

*(indicating Bor)*

*(Bor rises)*

*(pushing Bor & Con SL, Dog
steps to Leo)*

*(hands Dog coins)*

*(indicating Bor)*

well. I humbly give you permission to depart.
*[he exits]*

LEONATO:
Till tomorrow, lords, farewell.

DON PEDRO:
We will not fail you. *[all exit]*

Benedick is seeking out Beatrice to tell her that he has fulfilled his promise to her. He asks Margaret to fetch Beatrice to him, and while he waits for her, he muses that he is incapable of expressing his love in the traditional manner.

Beatrice arrives and asks, "What hath passed between you and Claudio?" Benedick informs her that he has indeed challenged Claudio. Benedick then turns the conversation to a discussion of their love for each other. After a playful exchange of wit, Benedick asks about Hero. At that moment, Margaret appears and tells them that everything has been resolved and that Beatrice should go to hear this news.

*[enter Benedick & Margaret]*
BENEDICK:
I beg you, sweet Mistress Margaret, do me a favor and fetch Beatrice so I may talk with her.

MARGARET:
Will you then write me a sonnet in praise of my beauty?

BENEDICK:
In the most lofty of styles, Margaret.

MARGARET:
Well then, I will call Beatrice to you. *[she exits]*

BENEDICK: *[reading]*
'The god of love,
That sits above
And knows me, and knows me,
How pitiful I deserve . . .'
Truly, I can't demonstrate it in rhyme, I've tried. I can find no rhyme to 'lady' but 'baby'—for 'scorn,' 'horn'—for 'school,' 'fool'—no, I was not born under a rhyming planet. *[enter Beatrice]* Sweet Beatrice, will you come when I call for you?

BEATRICE:
Yes, signior, and depart when you tell me.

| Act Five · Scene 1 **original abridged** | Act Five · Scene 1 **stage directions** |
|---|---|
| well. I humbly give you leave to depart. *[he exits]* | *(taking Con & exiting DL, Watch follow)* |
| LEONATO:<br>Until tomorrow, lords, farewell. | *(gesturing for Bor to follow, exits UC, Ant & Sext follow)* |
| DON PEDRO:<br>We will not fail. *[all exit]* | *(DP & Cl exit SL)* |

| Act Five · Scene 2 **original abridged** | Act Five · Scene 2 **stage directions** |
|---|---|
| *[enter Benedick & Margaret]*<br>BENEDICK:<br>Pray thee, sweet Mistress Margaret, deserve well at my hands by helping me to the speech of Beatrice. | *(enter UC, Mar R of Ben, Ben has removed sword, he holds sonnet, they X to RC)* |
| MARGARET:<br>Will you then write me a sonnet in praise of my beauty? | |
| BENEDICK:<br>In high style, Margaret. | |
| MARGARET:<br>Well, I will call Beatrice to you. *[she exits]* | *(exits SR, Ben X to UL bench, sits)* |
| BENEDICK: *[reading]*<br>'The god of love,<br>That sits above<br>And knows me, and knows me,<br>How pitiful I deserve...'<br>Marry, I cannot show it in rhyme; I have tried. I can find no rhyme to 'lady' but 'baby'—for 'scorn,' 'horn'—for 'school,' 'fool'—no, I was not born under a rhyming planet. *[enter Beatrice]* Sweet Beatrice, wouldst thou come when I called thee? | *(reads his sonnet in a 'sing-songy' style)*<br><br>*(Bea enters SR, X to RC, Ben rises)* |
| BEATRICE:<br>Yea, signior, and depart when you bid me. | *(curtsying)* |

BENEDICK:
Oh, stay until then!

BEATRICE:
'Then' is spoken; fare you well. And yet
before I go, give me what I came for, which
is to find out what transpired between you
and Claudio.

BENEDICK:
Only foul words—and therefore I will
kiss you.

BEATRICE:
Foul words are simply foul wind, and
foul wind is simply foul breath and
foul breath stinks; therefore I will
depart unkissed.

BENEDICK:
You have twisted the words from their
meaning, so forceful is your wit. But I
must plainly tell you, I have challenged
Claudio, and either I must hear from him
shortly, or I will proclaim him a coward.
And now I beg you to tell me, for which
of my bad qualities did you first fall in
love with me?

BEATRICE:
For them altogether, which maintained so
perfect a balance of evil that they will
not allow any good qualities to mix with
them. But for which of my good qualities
did you first suffer the pangs of love for me?

BENEDICK:
'Suffer love'—a good way to put it. I do
suffer love indeed, for I love you against
my will.

BEATRICE:
You are thwarting your own heart, I think.
Alas, poor heart! If you thwart it for loving
me, I will thwart it too—for I could never
love something my friend hates.

| Act Five · Scene 2   **original abridged** | Act Five · Scene 2   **stage directions** |
|---|---|

BENEDICK:
O, stay but till then!

BEATRICE:
'Then' is spoken; fare you well. And yet ere I go, let me go with that I came for, which is with knowing what hath passed between you and Claudio.

*(turns to leave, then turns back)*

BENEDICK:
Only foul words—and thereupon I will kiss thee.

*(X to Bea)*

BEATRICE:
Foul words is but foul wind, and foul wind is but foul breath, and foul breath is noisome; therefore I will depart un-kissed.

*(putting her hand up to stop him)*

*(turns to go)*

BENEDICK:
Thou hast frighted the word out of his right sense, so forcible is thy wit. But I must tell thee plainly, Claudio under-goes my challenge, and either I must shortly hear from him, or I will sub-scribe him a coward. And I pray thee now tell me, for which of my bad parts didst thou first fall in love with me?

*(Bea stops)*

*(Bea turns back to Ben)*

*(kisses Ben after 'coward,' then Ben 'escorts' Bea DRC)*

BEATRICE:
For them altogether, which maintained so politic a state of evil that they will not admit any good part to intermingle with them. But for which of my good parts did you first suffer love for me?

BENEDICK:
'Suffer love'—a good epithet. I do suffer love indeed, for I love thee against my will.

BEATRICE:
In spite of your heart, I think. Alas, poor heart! If you spite it for my sake, I will spite it for yours—for I will never love that which my friend hates.

**Act Five · Scene 2**     **vernacular**

BENEDICK:
You and I are too wise to woo peacefully.

BEATRICE:
It doesn't appear in this confession; there isn't one wise man in twenty who will praise himself.

BENEDICK:
An old, an old saying, Beatrice. These days, if a man does not erect his own tomb before he dies, he will be remembered no longer than the death bell rings and his widow weeps. But so much for praising myself, who I myself will swear is praiseworthy. And now tell me, how is your cousin?

BEATRICE:
Very ill.

BENEDICK:
And how are you?

BEATRICE:
Very ill too.

BENEDICK:
Serve God, love me, and be well. With that I leave you, for here comes someone in haste.

*[enter Ursula]*
URSULA:
Madam, you must come to your uncle. It has been proven that my Lady Hero was falsely accused, the Prince and Claudio greatly abused, and Don John is the cause of it all. Will you come quickly?

BEATRICE:
Will you go hear this news, signior?

BENEDICK:
I will live in your heart, lose my life in your lap, and be buried in your eyes; and also, I will go with you to your uncle's.
*[they exit]*

| Act Five · Scene 2  **original abridged** | Act Five · Scene 2  **stage directions** |
|---|---|
| BENEDICK:<br>Thou and I are too wise to woo peaceably. | *(taking Bea's hands)* |
| BEATRICE:<br>It appears not in this confession; there's not one wise man among twenty that will praise himself. | |
| BENEDICK:<br>An old, an old instance, Beatrice. If a man do not erect in this age his own tomb ere he dies, he shall live no longer in monument than the bell rings and the widow weeps. So much for praising myself, who I myself will bear witness is praise-worthy. And now tell me, how doth your cousin? | *(Xing DC)*<br><br><br><br><br>*(turning back to Bea)* |
| BEATRICE:<br>Very ill. | |
| BENEDICK:<br>And how do you? | *(Xing back to Bea)* |
| BEATRICE:<br>Very ill too. | |
| BENEDICK:<br>Serve God, love me, and mend. There will I leave you, for here comes one in haste. | *(taking her hands again)* |
| *[enter Ursula]*<br>URSULA:<br>Madam, you must come to your uncle. It is proved my Lady Hero hath been falsely accused, the Prince and Claudio mightily abused, and Don John is the author of all. Will you come presently? | *(Ur enters UC)*<br><br><br><br><br>*(Ur exits UC)* |
| BEATRICE:<br>Will you go hear this news, signior? | |
| BENEDICK:<br>I will live in thy heart, die in thy lap, and be buried in thy eyes; and moreover, I will go with thee to thy uncle's. *[they exit]* | *(after 'eyes' Ben kisses Bea)*<br><br>*(they exit UC)* |

## Act Five · Scene 3    scene analysis

This scene begins with Friar Francis, Leonato, and Benedick expressing their pleasure at the way things have turned out. Leonato reminds everyone that the Prince and Claudio should be arriving at any moment and sends the ladies off to don masks and return when they are called for.

Benedick asks the friar to perform a marriage ceremony for him and Beatrice. The friar and Leonato both consent to Benedick's request.

Claudio and the Prince enter, and when Claudio tells Leonato that he is still determined to marry Antonio's daughter, Leonato sends for the ladies. Claudio is presented with the lady he is to wed, and he agrees to marry her sight unseen. At this point, Hero removes her mask and Claudio is stunned. The friar tells him that he will explain everything after the ceremony is performed.

Benedick then asks to see Beatrice. Beatrice reveals herself, and Benedick proceeds to ask her if she is in love with him. When she denies she is, Benedick tells her that the Prince, Claudio, and Leonato have been deceived because they had been told that she was.

Beatrice then asks Benedick if he loves her. When he denies that he does, Beatrice tells him that her cousin, Margaret, and Ursula were deceived into believing that he did. When the others produce sonnets containing evidence of their love, they agree to take one another. Before proceeding to the church, Benedick insists they have a dance to lighten their hearts and their wives' heels.

## Act Five · Scene 3    vernacular

*[enter Leonato, Antonio, Benedick, Hero, Beatrice, Margaret, Ursula, Friar Francis]*
FRIAR FRANCIS:
Didn't I tell you she was innocent?

LEONATO:
So are the Prince and Claudio, who accused her.

ANTONIO:
Well, I am glad all these things turned out so well.

BENEDICK:
And so am I, otherwise I should have been obliged to make Claudio answer for it.

LEONATO:
The Prince and Claudio promised to visit me at this time. Daughter, and you young ladies, go inside, and when I send for you, come back masked. *[ladies exit]*

BENEDICK:
Friar, I must ask your help, I think.

FRIAR FRANCIS:
To do what, signior?

BENEDICK:
To tie the knot that binds, or undo me— one of them. Signior Leonato, the truth is, good signior, your niece looks upon me with a favorable eye.

LEONATO:
My daughter lent her that eye—it's very true.

BENEDICK:
And I requite her with the look of love.

| Act Five·Scene 3  **original abridged** | Act Five·Scene 3    **stage directions** |
|---|---|

| | |
|---|---|
| *[enter Leonato, Antonio, Benedick, Hero, Beatrice, Margaret, Ursula, Friar Francis]* | *(Leo & FF enter UC, FF R of Leo, X C, Ant & Ben follow, Ant X to R of FF, Ben X DR of Ant, Bea, Her, Mar & Ur follow, stopping US of the men in a cluster)* |
| FRIAR FRANCIS:<br>Did I not tell you she was innocent? | |
| LEONATO:<br>So are the Prince and Claudio, who accused her. | |
| ANTONIO:<br>Well, I am glad that all things sort so well. | |
| BENEDICK:<br>And so am I, being else by faith enforced to call young Claudio to a reckoning for it. | |
| LEONATO:<br>The Prince and Claudio promised by this hour to visit me. Daughter, and you gentlewomen, withdraw into a chamber, and when I send for you, come hither masked. *[ladies exit]* | *(ladies exit SR)* |
| BENEDICK:<br>Friar, I must entreat your pains, I think. | *(Xing to FF, Ant counters R)* |
| FRIAR FRANCIS:<br>To do what, signior? | |
| BENEDICK:<br>To bind me, or undo me—one of them. Signior Leonato, truth it is, good signior, your niece regards me with an eye of favor. | |
| LEONATO:<br>That eye my daughter lent her—'tis most true. | *(Xing DL 2 or 3 steps)* |
| BENEDICK:<br>And I do with an eye of love requite her. | *(Xing to Leo)* |

**Act Five • Scene 3** — **vernacular**

LEONATO:
That look I think you got from me, from Claudio and the Prince. But what is it you wish?

BENEDICK:
Your answer, sir, is puzzling. But as to what I wish, my wish is, that your good wishes go with us, so that today we may be joined in the honorable state of marriage; to which end, good friar, I shall need your help.

LEONATO:
My heart goes along with your wishes.

FRIAR FRANCIS:
And my help. *[enter Don Pedro & Claudio]* Here comes the Prince and Claudio.

DON PEDRO:
Good morning to this fine group.

LEONATO:
Good morning, Prince; good morning, Claudio. Are you still determined to marry my brother's daughter?

CLAUDIO:
My mind is made up.

LEONATO:
The friar's ready. Call her in.
*[Antonio exits then reenters with the masked ladies]*

CLAUDIO:
Which is the lady I must take as my own?

ANTONIO:
This is she.

CLAUDIO:
My dear, let me see your face.

LEONATO:
The sight whereof I think you had from me, from Claudio and the Prince. But what's your will?

BENEDICK:
Your answer, sir, is enigmatical. But for my will, my will is, your good will may stand with ours, this day to be conjoined in the state of honorable marriage; in which, good friar, I shall desire your help.

LEONATO:
My heart is with your liking.

FRIAR FRANCIS:
And my help. *[enter Don Pedro & Claudio]* Here comes the Prince and Claudio.

DON PEDRO:
Good morrow to this fair assembly.

LEONATO:
Good morrow, Prince; good morrow, Claudio. Are you yet determined to marry with my brother's daughter?

CLAUDIO:
I hold my mind.

LEONATO:
Here's the friar ready. Call her forth. *[Antonio exits then reenters with the masked ladies]*

CLAUDIO:
Which is the lady I must seize upon?

ANTONIO:
This same is she.

CLAUDIO:
Sweet, let me see your face.

*(FF X D to SR of Ben, DP & Cl enter DL & stop, Cl is SL of DP)*

*(Ant X to SR, signals offstage, ladies enter veiled Xing RC in a line, Ant stand DR of ladies)*

*(Xing DC)*

*(Ant brings Her to Cl, then X back to where he was)*

LEONATO:
No, You shall not till you take her
hand and swear to marry her before this
friar.

CLAUDIO:
Give me your hand before this holy friar.
I'll be your husband if you like me.

HERO: *[unmasking]*
And when I lived, I was your other wife—
and when you loved, you were my other
husband.

CLAUDIO:
Another Hero!

HERO:
Without a doubt. One Hero died defiled,
but I do live, and as sure as I am alive,
I am a virgin.

DON PEDRO:
The former Hero! Hero that is dead!

LEONATO:
She died, my lord, only while her slander
lived.

FRIAR FRANCIS:
I can lessen your amazement. After the
wedding, I'll tell you all about fair
Hero's death. Let's go to the chapel
immediately.

BENEDICK:
Just a minute friar. Which is Beatrice?

BEATRICE: *[unmasking]*
I answer to that name. What can I do for
you?

BENEDICK:
Do you not love me?

BEATRICE:
Why no—no more than is reasonable.

Act Five · Scene 3    **original abridged**

Act Five · Scene 3    **stage directions**

LEONATO:
No, that you shall not till you take her hand before this friar and swear to marry her.

*(taking a step DS)*

*(FF takes 2 steps DS to US of Her & Cl)*

CLAUDIO:
Give me your hand before this holy friar. I am your husband if you like of me.

HERO: *[unmasking]*
And when I lived, I was your other wife— and when you loved, you were my other husband.

*(removes her veil)*

CLAUDIO:
Another Hero!

HERO:
Nothing certainer. One Hero died defiled, but I do live, and surely as I live, I am a maid.

DON PEDRO:
The former Hero! Hero that is dead!

LEONATO:
She died, my lord, but whiles her slander lived.

FRIAR FRANCIS:
All this amazement can I qualify. After that the holy rites are ended, I'll tell you largely of fair Hero's death. To the chapel let us presently.

BENEDICK:
Soft and fair, friar. Which is Beatrice?

*(before anyone can move, Xing to ladies)*

BEATRICE: *[unmasking]*
I answer to that name. What is your will?

*(removes her veil & X to Ben)*

BENEDICK:
Do not you love me?

*(taking Bea DRC)*

BEATRICE:
Why no—no more than reason.

*(appropriate ad libs from others)*

BENEDICK:
Why then, your uncle, the Prince, and
Claudio have been deceived—they swore
you did.

BEATRICE:
Do you not love me?

BENEDICK:
Truly no—no more than is reasonable.

BEATRICE:
Why then, my cousin, Margaret and Ursula
are quite deceived—for they did swear you
did.

BENEDICK:
They swore that you were almost sick for
me.

BEATRICE:
They swore that you were nearly dead
for me.

BENEDICK:
It's no such thing. Then you do not
love me?

BEATRICE:
No, truly, but as a friend.

LEONATO:
Come on, cousin, I am sure you love the
gentleman.

CLAUDIO:
And I will swear that he loves her, for
here is a paper in his own writing, a
lamely written sonnet created for Beatrice
from his own pure brain.

HERO:
And here's another, in my cousin's
handwriting, stolen from her pocket,
about her affection for Benedick.

| Act Five·Scene 3 **original abridged** | Act Five·Scene 3    **stage directions** |
|---|---|

**BENEDICK:**
Why then, your uncle, and the Prince, and Claudio have been deceived—they swore you did.

**BEATRICE:**
Do not you love me?

**BENEDICK:**
Troth no—no more than reason.

*(more ad libs)*

**BEATRICE:**
Why then, my cousin, Margaret and Ursula are much deceived—for they did swear you did.

**BENEDICK:**
They swore that you were almost sick for me.

**BEATRICE:**
They swore that you were well-nigh dead for me.

**BENEDICK:**
'Tis no such matter. Then you do not love me?

**BEATRICE:**
No, truly, but in friendly recompense.

**LEONATO:**
Come, cousin, I am sure you love the gentleman.

*(Xing DS a step)*

**CLAUDIO:**
And I'll be sworn that he loves her, for here's a paper written in his hand, a halting sonnet of his own pure brain, fashioned to Beatrice.

*(Xing DS around Her to Bea & Ben holding up sonnet, Bea grabs it from his hand)*

**HERO:**
And here's another, writ in my cousin's hand, stolen from her pocket, containing her affection unto Benedick.

*(Her X to L of Cl, holds sonnet out DS of Cl, Ben grabs it)*

**Act Five · Scene 3          vernacular**

BENEDICK:
A miracle! Here are our written words in
direct contrast to our hearts. Come, I'll
have you—but, by this light, I take you
for pity.

BEATRICE:
I won't reject you—but, by this good
day, I give in because of great persuasion,
and partly to save your life—for I was
told you were wasting away.

BENEDICK:
Hush! I will stop your mouth. *[he kisses
her]*

DON PEDRO:
How are you Benedick—'the married
man'?

BENEDICK:
I'll tell you what, Prince, since I do
intend to marry, I will ignore anything
the world has to say against it; and
therefore don't throw up to me what I
have said against it; for man is a giddy
thing, and this is my conclusion. For
your part, Claudio, I thought I was going
to have to beat you, but since we are
likely to be related, live unbruised and
love my cousin. Come on, come on, let's be
friends. Let's have a dance before we are
wed to lighten our hearts and our wives'
heels. Play music! Prince, you look sad.
Get yourself a wife, get yourself a wife!
Strike up the music! *[all dance]*

Finis

| Act Five·Scene 3 **original abridged** | Act Five·Scene 3    **stage directions** |
|---|---|

BENEDICK:
A miracle! Here's our own hands against our hearts. Come, I will have thee—but, by this light, I take thee for pity.

*(Bea & Ben perusing the sonnets)*

BEATRICE:
I would not deny you—but, by this good day, I yield upon great persuasion, and partly to save your life—for I was told you were in a consumption.

BENEDICK:
Peace! I will stop your mouth. *[he kisses her]*

*(Ben kisses Bea)*

DON PEDRO:
How dost thou, Benedick, 'the married man'?

*(Xing R a few steps)*

BENEDICK:
I'll tell thee what, Prince, since I do purpose to marry, I will think nothing to any purpose that the world can say against it; and therefore never flout at me for what I have said against it; for man is a giddy thing, and this is my conclusion. For thy part, Claudio, I did think to have beaten thee, but in that thou art like to be my kinsman, live unbruised and love my cousin. Come, come, we are friends. Let's have a dance ere we are married that we may lighten our hearts and our wives' heels. Play music! Prince, thou art sad. Get thee a wife, get thee a wife! Strike up pipers! *[all dance]*

*(arm around Bea)*

*(music plays, all take hands & dance)*

Finis

(We have selected our punctuation based on the First Folio and Staunton's "The Plays of Shakespeare" (1858–1861). We have taken some minor liberties with Shakespeare's text to accommodate our abridged version and for this we apologize to purists, to scholars and, most of all, to Shakespeare!)

# "His words are a very fantastical banquet"

A DISCUSSION OF THE LANGUAGE IN SHAKESPEARE'S PLAYS

Having read the play, let's take a little time to look at Shakespeare's language—very different from the way we speak today!

Language evolves over the course of time. Foreign influences, developments in technology, new slang, and altered usages of words all affect the way we communicate. What is perfectly clear in 1998 might be almost incomprehensible by the year 2398.

At the time that Shakespeare wrote, English was evolving at a particularly furious pace. In 1066, England had been conquered by Frenchmen (Normans) who made French the official language of England. The upper classes spoke French; the lower classes spoke English (which was at that time a kind of German called Saxon), while all church business was conducted in Latin.

Over the course of time, a melding of these languages occurred. And along with this came a new national identity and pride. The inhabitants of England no longer thought of themselves as Saxons or Frenchmen but as Englishmen.

By the time Henry V reestablished English as the official language of the land around 1400, English was evolving into a new and extremely exciting vehicle for communication. New words and new ways of saying things became the mark of a clever person.

It was into this atmosphere that Shakespeare was born. By the time Shakespeare had come along, language was not merely a tool used to get through the day, but a song to be sung, a flag to be waved, capable of expressing anything and everything. It was a kind of national sport. The basic rules had been laid down, and now the sky was the limit. Everyone was a rapper, a wordsmith. And Shakespeare was better at this game than anyone of his time and perhaps since. It is said that Shakespeare added over a thousand new words to the language.

Getting easy with Shakespeare is like learning to read or drive; once you get the hang of it, your world is changed. Language is the guardian at the entrance gate to the land of Shakespeare. To enter, one must tame the guardian. This simply means that you must take the time to become familiar with his ways. And now for the good news, once you learn the guardian's ways, he changes. He ceases to be an obstacle and instead becomes your guide and ally; your conveyance to Shakespeare's world and mind.

Let's examine a few of the techniques that will help you to tame the guardian and make your exploration of Shakespeare easier.

1. The first thing to do is to find out what all the words mean. To do this, you will want to go to your local library and gather any Shakespeare lexicons or glossaries, and as many different dictionaries and thesauri as you can locate, along with all the versions of *Much Ado* that they have (with all their various footnotes and explanations). Then look up all the words you don't know. Note their various meanings and try to determine which best fits the context you found the word in.

2. We must remember that Shakespeare (as well as other poets) takes poetic license; he allows himself to deviate from accepted form to achieve a desired effect. Poets will often rearrange words to achieve a more musical, poetical structure, or perhaps to get a rhyme to occur at the end of a line. Sometimes, by merely rearranging the subject, verb, adverbs, etc., of a complicated sentence, we can more easily understand its meaning.

For example, in Act 4 scene 1 when the friar says, "Your daughter here the princes left for dead," this line may seem somewhat confusing at first glance, but if we rearrange the words to read, "The princes left your daughter here for dead," it seems perfectly clear.

In Act 4 scene 2, the Sexton's line, "What heard you him say else?," can be clarified by simply turning the phrase around to read, "What else did you hear him say?" (Note that we also changed "heard you" to "did you hear" to keep our tenses straight.)

By changing Shakespeare's language, his poetry is often sacrificed, so always remember to go back to the original.

3. Shakespeare also takes words and stretches their obvious meanings. He will use a word in a correct but somewhat unusual manner to make us see something in a whole new light.

When Benedick says, "For my part, I am so attired in wonder, I know not what to say," in Act 4 scene 1, Shakespeare is having him use the word *attired* in a rather unique way.

We generally think of the word in terms of being dressed or clothed, but rarely do we think of it as Shakespeare uses it here. Shakespeare has taken the idea of attired and stretched its meaning to include the idea of being able to wear an attitude. So when Benedick says he is attired in wonder, he is saying that he is wearing his wonderment or that he is amazed.

Another example of Shakespeare stretching a meaning can be found in the line, "The word is too good to paint out her wickedness."

With this line, Don John is saying that the word *disloyal* is too polite a word to fully represent or describe Hero's wicked character. Shakespeare has here stretched the meaning of the word *paint* to make us see words being used as picture-making tools to describe Hero's disloyalty.

When we come across a situation like this, we must look at the context of the unusual usage and use our imaginations to stretch the meanings of the word as Shakespeare might have done. Once we start thinking like Shakespeare, we can open ourselves to the various shades of meaning contained in words.

4. Shakespeare's use of the apostrophe sometimes makes words seem strange to us, but when we realize that he is using it no differently than we do in modern English, the words become easy to understand.

An apostrophe merely tells us that there is something missing. For example in the word *I'll*, the apostrophe replaces the *w* and the *i;* "I'll" is a contraction for "I will." So with Shakespeare, the word *'tis* means "it is" and *ta'en* means "taken." Shakespeare often contracts words in this manner to alter the number of syllables in a line in order to fit his poetic structure.

5. Yet another thing to keep in mind when dealing with Shakespeare is that most of the punctuation in the versions you will read was put there by an editor in subsequent centuries and was not Shakespeare's.

Quite frankly, Shakespeare was more concerned with meaning than with grammatically correct punctuation. He was writing for actors, and his objective with punctuation was to clarify how an actor should interpret a line. In fact, it is thought that many of the actors in Shakespeare's company could not read and the learning of a script was a verbal process.

Therefore, a good way to get more comfortable with Shakespeare might be to listen to professional actors on recordings of Shakespeare's plays and follow along in a script. Don't be afraid to imitate what you hear; it is an excellent way to learn.

6. We find, though, that the very best way to become comfortable with Shakespeare and his language is to work with the material out loud. There is something marvelous that happens when we say the words aloud that helps to clarify their meanings.

Merely reading about baseball rarely improves your batting average—so with Shakespeare. His material was meant to be performed, and therefore, the best way to connect to and understand the material is to speak it out loud, preferably with other people—but even alone works wonders.

You'll be amazed to discover Shakespeare's language becoming clearer and clearer as you work this way. Just remember: patience and practice!

# Taming the guardian

AN EXERCISE TO HELP UNDERSTAND SHAKESPEARE'S LANGUAGE

This exercise is designed to put into practice the various techniques for understanding Shakespeare that we have just talked about.

Select one of the following speeches (which are from *Much Ado* and have either been cut or not used in their entirety in our version of the play) and translate the speech into vernacular American English.

This is the time to go to the library and locate all those reference books and look up all the words in the speech you've chosen. You might want to do this working as a group or in pairs, sharing your ideas as you work, or you might work individually on the same speech, and then compare results after.

Once you have found the various meanings of the words and made lists of them, you can begin to select the ones that seem most appropriate for conveying the meaning of the speech. Note that you may also need to rearrange the word order to clarify the meaning.

Now put this all together and write a vernacular version of the speech. When doing this, try to imagine the words that the character who speaks the speech in the play might use if he or she were speaking today.

Remember, there are no right or wrong ways to do this exercise. Be creative and daring. Shakespeare certainly would be if he were around today and had our version of the English language to work with!

Now that you have broken the code and the guardian is starting to seem friendlier, go back to the original version of your speech and read it aloud, strongly keeping in mind the meanings of the words that you have now discovered. Note how much clearer Shakespeare's language has become for you and for your listeners. This is what every actor knows: the clearer the understanding of the language, the more clearly it will be conveyed.

Note, too, how well Shakespeare says things—in such a way that pretty much sums it up. It is not only the words he chooses, but the order he has selected to put them in that creates the incredibly rich imagery that he is so famous for. It's interesting, too, to see how many words it can take to translate Shakespeare's succinct images into vernacular American. You could say it differently, perhaps, but not better! It is possible to update the language with vernacular versions, but it is certainly never preferable to use them for any reason other than as a tool for getting back to the original. He is the MASTER! And now that you are learning how to tame the guardian, you will be able enter into

Shakespeare's world and begin to discover the breadth and depth of his insights into human nature.

You will note that for this exercise, we have printed Shakespeare's text in verse form when it appears that way in the original. We have chosen not to use the verse form in our cut version for reasons of simplicity, but now that you have become more familiar with Shakespeare and his language, it might be a good idea to get used to it.

When dealing with the verse form:

1. Do not stop at the end of the line unless there is punctuation telling you to.
2. If there is no period or other punctuation, continue reading on until the thought is complete.
3. Don't be thrown by the fact that each line begins with a capitalized letter; this is merely part of the form.

Some of the following text is printed as ordinary prose; that is how it appears in the original. Shakespeare often switched back and forth between verse and prose depending on the effect he wished to accomplish.

BEATRICE: (Act 1 scene 1, telling why Benedick should be grateful for the tiny capacity of wit he has remaining after the rest abandoned him following their last encounter)

In our last conflict, four of his five wits went halting off, and now is the whole man governed with one; so that if he have wit enough to keep himself warm, let him bear it for a difference between himself and his horse; for it is all the wealth that he hath left to be known a reasonable creature.

BENEDICK: (Act 1 scene 1, telling Don Pedro how armored he is against any attacks of love)

With anger, with sickness, or with hunger, my lord; not with love. Prove that ever I lose more blood with love than I will get again with drinking, pick out mine eyes with a ballad-maker's pen and hang me up at the door of a brothel house for the sign of blind Cupid.

BENEDICK: (Act 1 scene 1, telling Don Pedro to look to his own flaws before pointing out those of others)

Nay, mock not, mock not. The body of your discourse is sometime guarded with fragments, and the guards are but slightly basted on neither. Ere you flout old ends any further, examine your conscience. And so I leave you.

DON PEDRO: (Act 1 scene 1, telling Claudio that he will assist him in his pursuit of Hero's hand)

Thou wilt be like a lover presently,
And tire the hearer with a book of words.
If thou dost love fair Hero, cherish it,
And I will break with her and with her father,
And thou shalt have her. Was't not to this end
That thou began'st to twist so fine a story?

DON JOHN: (Act 1 scene 3, telling Conrade the dirty low-down about himself)

. . . it better fits my blood to be disdained of all than to fashion a carriage to rob love from any. In this, though I cannot be said to be a flattering honest man, it must not be denied but I am a plain-dealing villain. I am trusted with a muzzle and enfranchised with a clog. Therefore I have decreed not to sing in my cage.

BEATRICE: (Act 2 scene 1, explaining why there is no man for her to marry)

He that hath a beard is more than a youth, and he that hath no beard is less than a man; and he that is more than a youth is not for me, and he that is less than a man, I am not for him.

BENEDICK: (Act 2 scene 3, telling of his dismay at Claudio's desire to "turn husband")

I have known when there was no music with him but the drum and the fife, and now had he rather hear the tabor and the pipe. I have known when he would have walked ten mile afoot to see a good armor, and now will he lie ten nights awake carving the fashion of a new doublet. He was wont to speak plain and to the purpose, like an honest man and a soldier, and now is he turned orthography, his words are a very fantastical banquet—just so many strange dishes.

CLAUDIO & LEONATO: (Act 2 scene 3, describing how desperately in love Beatrice is)

CLAUDIO:
Then down upon her knees she falls, weeps, sobs, beats her heart, tears her hair, prays, curses— 'O sweet Benedick! God give me patience!'

LEONATO:
She doth indeed, my daughter says so, and the ecstasy hath so much overborne her that my daughter is sometime afeard she will do a desperate outrage to herself. It is very true.

LEONATO: (Act 2 scene 3, expressing his distress over Beatrice's supposed love for Benedick)

Oh my lord, wisdom and blood combating in so tender a body, we have ten proofs to one that blood hath the victory. I am sorry for her, as I have just cause, being her uncle and her guardian.

CLAUDIO: (Act 2 scene 3, reinforcing the extent of Beatrice's love for Benedick)

Hero thinks surely she will die; for she says she will die if he love her not, and she will die ere she make her love known, and she will die if he woo her, rather than she will bate one breath of her accustomed crossness.

DON PEDRO: (Act 2 scene 3, looking ahead to Beatrice and Benedick's first meeting after their gullings)

Let there be the same net spread for her, and that must your daughter and her gentlewomen carry. The sport will be when they hold one an opinion of another's dotage, and no such matter. That's the scene that I would see, which will be merely a dumb show. Let us send her to call him in to dinner.

HERO: (Act 3 scene 1, telling Margaret what to say in order to set Beatrice up for her gulling scene)

Say that thou overheard'st us,
And bid her steal into the pleached bower,
Where honeysuckles, ripened by the sun,
Forbid the sun to enter, like favorites
Made proud by princes, that advance their pride
Against that power that bred it. There will she
   hide her
To listen our propose. This is thy office.
Bear thee well in it and leave us alone.

HERO: (Act 3 scene 1, describing how Beatrice treats gentlemen who try to court her)

             If fair-faced,
She would swear the gentleman should be her sister;
If black, why nature, drawing of an antic,
Made a foul blot; if tall, a lance ill-headed;
If low, an agate very vilely cut;
If speaking, why, a vane blown with all winds;
If silent, why, a block moved with none.
So turns she every man the wrong side out
And never gives to truth and virtue that
Which simpleness and merit purchaseth.

DON PEDRO: (Act 3 scene 2, talking about Benedick and his capacity to outwit love)

. . . for from the crown of his head to the sole of his foot, he is all mirth. He hath twice or thrice cut Cupid's bowstring, and the little hangman dare

not shoot at him. He hath a heart as sound as a bell, and his tongue is the clapper, for what his heart thinks, his tongue speaks.

DON JOHN: (Act 3 scene 2, ensnaring Claudio in his plot to discredit Hero)

You may think I love you not. Let that appear hereafter, and aim better at me by that I now will manifest. For my brother, I think he holds you well, and in dearness of heart hath holp to effect your ensuing marriage—surely suit ill spent and labor ill bestowed.

DOGBERRY & VERGES: (Act 3 scene 3, debating the finer points of the law)

DOGBERRY:
If you meet the Prince in the night, you may stay him.

VERGES:
Nay, by'r lady, that I think 'a cannot.

DOGBERRY:
Five shillings to one on't with any man that knows the statutes, he may stay him. Marry, not without the Prince be willing—for indeed the watch ought to offend no man, and it is an offence to stay a man against his will.

CLAUDIO: (Act 4 scene 1, renouncing Hero and locking his heart to the temptations of love)

Oh Hero! what a Hero hadst thou been
If half thy outward graces had been placed
About thy thoughts and counsels of thy heart!
But fare thee well, most foul, most fair; farewell,
Thou pure impiety and impious purity.
For thee I'll lock up all the gates of love,
And on my eyelids shall conjecture hang,
To turn all beauty into thoughts of harm,
And never shall it more be gracious.

LEONATO: (Act 4 scene 1, arguing with the friar as to Hero's innocence)

             Friar, it cannot be.
Thou seest that all the grace that she hath left
Is that she will not add to her damnation
A sin of perjury—she not denies it.
Why seek'st thou then to cover with excuse
That which appears in proper nakedness?

LEONATO: (Act 4 scene 1, avowing that he is not yet so old or without means to exact revenge upon those who have dishonored Hero if that proves to be the case)

Time hath not yet so dried this blood of mine,
Nor age so eat up my invention,

Nor fortune made such havoc of my means,
Nor my bad life reft me so much of friends,
But they shall find awaked in such a kind
Both strength of limb and policy of mind,
Ability in means, and choice of friends,
To quit me of them throughly.

FRIAR FRANCIS: (Act 4 scene 1, counting on Claudio's humanity to cause him to repent when he hears of Hero's death)
When he shall hear she died upon his words,
The idea of her life shall sweetly creep
Into his study of imagination.
And every lovely organ of her life
Shall come appareled in more precious habit,
More moving, delicate, and full of life,
Into the eye and prospect of his soul
Than when she lived indeed.

LEONATO: (Act 5 scene 1, disdaining the effectiveness of philosophy to dispel grief)
Measure his woe the length and breadth of mine,
And let it answer every strain for strain,
As thus for thus, and such a grief for such,
In every lineament, branch, shape, and form.
If such a one will smile and stroke his beard,
Bid sorrow wag, cry 'hem' when he should groan,
Patch grief with proverbs, make misfortune drunk
With candle-wasters—bring him yet to me
And I of him will gather patience.

ANTONIO: (Act 5 scene 1, putting down so-called honorable men as paper tigers)
I know them, yea,
And what they weigh, even to the utmost scruple,
Scambling, outfacing, fashion-monging boys,
That lie, and cog, and flout, deprave, and slander,
Go anticly, and show outward hideousness,
And speak off half a dozen dang'rous words,
How they might hurt their enemies, if they durst,
And this is all.

# "There's a double meaning in that"

MORE LANGUAGE EXERCISES

These exercises are designed to help familiarize you with Shakespeare's words and to illustrate how similar they are to our current English language.

The following list contains words and phrases from *Much Ado* along with their modern equivalents.

Using these words and phrases:

1. Write a letter from your character in the play to another character and use at least ten of the words or phrases in your letter.
2. Whenever possible, try to incorporate these words and phrases into your discussions of the play in class.
3. Sneak these words and phrases into conversation when speaking to your family or friends and see how they react. Can you work the phrase into conversation so that they understand you without your having to explain what you mean?

| *Shakespeare's words* | *Modern English* |
|---|---|
| none of name | no one important |
| sworn brother | best friend |
| nobody marks you | no one's listening |
| in what key | in what sense |
| see without spectacles | see clearly, be astute |
| in sport | kidding |
| is't come to this? | is that how it is? |
| in faith | truly |
| held you here | kept you here |
| to fetch me in | to trick me, to trap me |
| by my troth | truly |
| the fine is | the upshot or conclusion is |
| fall from this faith | waiver, change one's mind |
| as time shall try | we'll see, time will tell |
| temporize with the hours | come round in time |
| repair to | go to (someplace) |
| commend me to | send my compliments to |
| dost thou | do you |
| break with | bring up, mention to, inform |
| fit thee with | equip you with, supply you with |
| revelling | partying |
| unclasp | reveal, open up |
| thine | yours |
| as the event stamps them | as time will tell |
| discovered | disclosed, told |
| accordant | in agreement |
| withal | with this, with it |
| what the goodyear | what the hell |
| have stomach | be hungry |
| of late | lately, recently |
| stood out against | opposed |
| ta'en | taken |
| frame the season for your own harvest | learn to act in your own best interests |
| newly | recently |
| hath | has |
| fits my blood | suits me |
| fashion a carriage | put on a front, pretend |

| | |
|---|---|
| give intelligence | inform, tell of |
| betroth oneself to unquietness | set yourself up for a bad time |
| start-up | upstart |
| shrewd of thy tongue | smart-mouthed |
| apprehend passing shrewdly | understand very well |
| break a comparison | make a wisecrack, crack a joke |
| strikes into melancholy | depresses |
| reputed | known to be |
| hath a quarrel | has a bone to pick |
| conference | conversation |
| lest | unless |
| conceit | belief, notion, idea |
| 'tis | it is, it's |
| I cry you mercy | I beg your pardon |
| look to | attend to, take care of |
| a sevennight | a week |
| in the interim | in the meantime |
| to fashion | to contrive, to make happen, to shape or design |
| tell you my drift | fill you in, tell you my plan |
| canst | can |
| thou | you |
| in favor | liked, approved of |
| stale | whore |
| instances | examples |
| ay | yes |
| is't? | is it? |
| past the infinite of thought | unbelievable, unimaginable |
| to counterfeit | to pretend |
| a gull | a trick, a trap |
| pretty jest | amusing story |
| make sport of | make fun of |
| out of all suspicion | unquestionably |
| bestow dotage | fall for |
| exceeding | very, extremely |
| let it cool the while | let things cool down |
| will you walk? | shall we go? |
| dote on | adore |
| doth | does |
| fair | pretty |
| bid | ask, beg |
| fear you not | don't worry |
| entreat | beg, implore |
| framed by | created by, made from |
| self-endeared | self-centered |
| every day tomorrow | from tomorrow on |
| limed | ensnared, trapped |
| dost | do |
| thither | there, to that place |
| vouchsafe | allow, permit |
| be bold with | presume upon |
| good den | good evening |
| hither | here |
| paint out | describe, express |
| bear it coldly | keep your cool |
| hobby-horses | jack-asses, jerks |
| didst | did |
| 'twas | it was |
| by my troth | truly, indeed |
| 'twill | it will, it'll |
| I warrant you | I promise you |
| wherefore? | why? |
| ope | open |
| would'st | would |
| attired in wonder | amazed |
| twelvemonth | year |
| tarry | stay, wait |
| thine | your |
| belied | lied about, falsely accused |
| have some haste | in a hurry |
| daff | dismiss, rebuff |
| shalt | shall |
| fain | gladly, willingly |
| high-proof | potently, extremely |
| in earnest | serious |
| hast | has |
| possess the people | tell everyone |
| ere | before |
| didst | did |
| well-nigh | nearly, almost |
| thy | your |
| thee | you |

# "In practice let us put it presently"

USING IMPROVISATION TO EXPLORE CHARACTERS

Actors often use a technique called improvisation for the purpose of discovering aspects of their characters that might not be immediately evident or accessible to them. We set up a situation—usually based on the play we are working on—and then act it out, making up words and actions on the spot. By doing this, we hope to achieve a deeper and more honest response to the circumstances and relationships that we are investigating. We then take this new understanding that we have discovered from the improv and incorporate it into our character when we return to our work on the actual script.

The following are suggestions for improvs that might be helpful when working on *Much Ado*.

1. Improv the scene between Leonato and Hero when he tells her that he has heard that the Prince is going to court her and instructs her how to respond. How does Hero react to this news?
2. Improv the scene between Don Pedro and Hero when he is courting her for Claudio.
3. Don Pedro "breaks with" Leonato about Claudio's desire to wed Hero. How does Leonato react? Remember, he thought the Prince was wooing Hero for himself.
4. Don Pedro sets up Benedick's gulling scene with Claudio and Leonato. Who is to do and say what to make it all work?
5. Don Pedro plans Beatrice's gulling scene with Hero.
6. Borachio convinces Margaret to participate in the charade at Hero's chamber window.
7. The scene that takes place at Hero's chamber window the night before the wedding (including all the onlookers).
8. Margaret convinces Beatrice to come out and overhear her gulling scene.
9. The Watch tells Dogberry about their arrest of Borachio and Conrade.
10. While Beatrice is spending the restless night after her gulling scene, what is she thinking and feeling? Do this as a monologue.
11. Think about the conversations that might take place between Beatrice, Hero, Leonato, and Antonio after the wedding and improv these.
12. Make up an improv that shows how the news of Don John's escape from Messina is spread through the town. You may have to create townspeople who are not actually in the play to make this one work. Who discovered that he'd left? When?
13. Benedick looks for Claudio to challenge him. What's going through Benedick's head as he goes to find Claudio? Verbalize his thoughts in a monologue.
14. The scene between the Sexton and Leonato when the Sexton reports the results of the examination of the prisoners.

# The rehearsal process

WHO'S WHO AND WHAT'S WHAT IN
PUTTING A PLAY TOGETHER

## WHO'S WHO

There is first of all the play, then the actors, then the director. The job of the director is to make sure the story gets told. This can entail many elements:

working with actors to help them develop their characters, making sure each actor is headed in the right direction, maintaining order in the rehearsal so that work can move along smoothly, assigning people to do props, costumes, etc. The director is ultimately the benign dictator who makes sure everything comes together at the right time–that's why they get the big bucks!

The stage manager is the director's right hand, a combination of sergeant at arms and girl Friday. The stage manager's many jobs include: recording the blocking in a master script, prompting the actors when they forget their lines (that means a stage manager must always be following along in the script during rehearsals), making sure everyone is at rehearsal on time, coordinating the technical elements (props, costumes, etc.), calling break times and gathering everyone together after the break, and helping the director maintain an orderly rehearsal. Once the show is in performance, the stage manager must make sure everyone and everything is in the proper place to ensure the show will run smoothly, and, most important, the stage manager must never become frazzled!

The stage manager can usually use an assistant or two. Give careful consideration when selecting someone for this position–a good stage manager is invaluable!

## CASTING THE PLAY

The first thing we need to do is to cast the play; that is, figure out who will play which role. This can be done by having auditions for the parts. To do this, people read various scenes from the play, and then the director, teacher, or the other members of the class determine who would be best suited to play a certain role.

Another way to cast is to have the teacher assign roles. Sometimes it is fun to have multiple casts (more than one actor for each part); that way actors can share their ideas in rehearsal and learn from each other.

With multiple casting, the play could then be presented more times in order to give everyone a chance to read or perform. Note too that a single actor might play more than one role. This is known as *doubling*. Doubling and double casting will depend on the number of actors available for your production.

Something to keep in mind when casting is that an obvious choice for a role may not always be the best one. Sometimes a male part might be better played by a female actor or vica versa. Or an actor whose physical characteristics are not exactly what's called for might actually be able to bring something more interesting to a certain part. So remember to be flexible and open-minded in the casting process.

## INVESTIGATING THE SCRIPT

Once the casting is determined, it's time to get to work. Professional actors usually begin the rehearsal process by sitting around together and reading the play out loud a number of times. The first time through, we just listen to the story. The next time through, we start discussing the play.

The rules here are usually that anyone may stop and ask a question at any time. It could be a question of the meaning of a word, a discussion of why a character does something, or perhaps a question about where a scene is taking place. In other words, everything and anything that may not be perfectly clear should be examined at this point. This is done to make sure that everyone fully understands what is being said and what is going on in the course of the play.

This can take days or even a week in a professional company (and that's working eight hours a day!). So take your time on this step and be thorough. The more time spent clarifying everything at this stage of the process, the more smoothly the rest of the rehearsal will go.

Once all the questions have been answered, go back and read the play again and note how much richer and clearer the language will be for you.

At this point the decision must be made whether you are going to do a reading of the play or a simple production. A *reading* is a modified performance in which there would be no sets or costumes and is usually done with only the simplest movement. Actors could just be seated in a semicircle, facing the listeners with their scripts in hand, and read the play.

## DOING A READING

If you have decided upon a reading, you still must determine how best to tell the story of the play to make it clear and interesting for the audience. This is done by adding *shape* or *structure* to our work. We do this by going scene-by-scene through the play and (having determined what the scene is about in our previous work) figuring out how it fits into the overall *arc* of the play, how that scene moves the story forward, and how each character contributes to that movement.

By examining the scenes in this way, we can then determine the *rhythms* that the scene requires for the acting of it: for example, some will need to be fast-paced, some slow, some a combination of both; some will need to be quiet, some raucous; in some, the characters will speak quickly—perhaps overlapping the previous speaker, and in others, the language will be languid or perhaps romantic. All these various elements will add what we refer to as *shape* and *color* to the material.

We do this with each scene and slowly expand our work to include larger sections, till the entire shape of the play becomes clear. Experiment, explore, and see what works best for your production. The director makes the final decisions because he or she will have the best overview of the play, having been able to watch it all.

The most important element for a reading is a clear understanding of the language, the situation (or story), and the character relationships. These are, after all, the most critical elements of Shakespeare.

This would be an excellent place for most classes to get to. But, for those of you who wish to do a simple staging of the play read on.

## BLOCKING

If you have decided to stage a production of the play, you still must do all the work of shaping discussed in the reading section, only you do this while *blocking* the play.

Blocking is the process of organizing the physical movement of the play. We usually block while working one scene at a time and holding our scripts (that is, before beginning to memorize our lines.) We do this because most actors find it much easier to memorize lines when the lines are connected to movements. (Note that the blocking we have offered with the text is merely one way to go, feel free to create movement that feels comfortable for you.)

## WORKING SCENES AND MEMORIZING

The next step would be to *work scenes* of the play—that is, to rehearse them, adjusting the blocking as needed to make sure the actors feel comfortable with the movement, and checking that the situations in the text are being properly clarified. It is during this step that we also begin memorizing the lines.

Memorization usually begins to happen on its own at this point, particularly if all the previous discussion work has been thoroughly accomplished. Shakespeare writes so well that his words seem to become the only ones to say in the situations that he has devised. This is not the case with all playwrights!

There are times though (particularly with longer speeches) when it is necessary to go over and over a section out loud until it is ingrained in the brain and in the muscles of the mouth. (It's amazing how many times on stage an actor has forgotten a line, but his or her mouth still keeps going and knows what to say!) If an actor forgets a line during rehearsal, he or she says the word *line* and the stage manager (who is following in the script) reads the line to the actor and work goes on.

This period of rehearsal is the longest and most exciting part of the process. It is when we go over and over each scene that the language and the actions truly become part of us and we grow to understand a little more about the characters and their situations each time through. It is over this period that it is often said we are *becoming* the character. In a professional situation, we are lucky if we have four weeks to spend on this part of the process. So again, spend as much time as you can.

Once individual scenes begin to take shape, we start putting together larger chunks of the play, perhaps doing three or four scenes in a row. It is now that we begin to feel the *flow* of the play and find the *throughline* of the characters.

Don't forget that this is an ongoing process and that different actors have creative inspirations at different points in the rehearsal period. If someone comes up with a new and exciting idea after blocking has been completed, experiment with it and be willing to change if it turns out to be better. This is the *creative process,* and these are the very instincts and ideas that will make your production unique and wonderful.

## RUN-THROUGHS

It is at this point that we put the whole play together and go through it from beginning to end. It is during the *run-throughs* that we finally get to understand what is needed from us as actors to take our character from his or her starting place to where he or she will end up in the play. Do as many run-throughs as your schedule permits, reworking any problem areas before or after the run-throughs.

## TECHS AND DRESSES

It is now that we add the final elements of props and costumes (sometimes we are lucky enough to have gotten these earlier in our rehearsal process and have been able to incorporate them sooner). But we definitely need everything at this point! These are referred to as the *technical* elements of the production.

Remember, though, that the ultimate element of any Shakespearean production is the incredibly wonderful language through which Shakespeare conveys his ideas. Keep it simple and clear and it will enlighten and uplift. . . . Good show!

# Developing a character

AN EXERCISE FOR CREATING A
CHARACTER HISTORY

When working on a play, an actor will usually create a *history* or *background* for his or her character. This is the story of the character's life. It is made up by

the actor to gather insights into the character's psyche and better understand how that character will respond to the various situations that he or she is confronted with in the course of a play.

We create this story by examining the *givens* in the text (that is, the various hints that the playwright has written into or given in the script) and making lists of all the information that we gather.

These include:

1. Everything that is said about the character by other characters in the play.
2. Everything the character says about him or herself.
3. An examination of the physical characteristics and the physical limitations that the playwright might have specified in the text.

In addition to this information, we get more by asking a series of questions about the character:

1. What does the character want? This is a twofold question:
   A. What does the character want in the big picture of life? Does he or she want to be a movie star? To be rich? To be loved?
   B. What does the character want in each scene? In other words, what is he or she desiring the other characters to do or say?
2. How does the character go about getting those things? Does the character aggressively go after things or is he or she passive? Will she "sell her grandmother"? Is he honest and plodding?
3. How does the character react in various situations? With anger? Passively? With compassion?
4. How does the character feel about him or herself?
5. What is his or her environment or social situation? Is this character from a family of fourteen and ignored by everyone? Is he or she from a big city? A small town? A rich family? A well-educated family?
6. How does the character's mind operate? Is he or she quick-witted or slow? Plodding or inventive?
7. What is the character's journey through the play? In other words, what is the character like when we first encounter him or her and when and how does the character evolve, grow, or change during the course of the play? Or does the character remain unchanged?

We find the answers to these questions by scouring the text and by creating answers with our imaginations when they are not available. This is precisely why no two actors can ever play a character the same way. Each actor has personally created that character!

We now take the givens we have discovered in the text and combine these with the various answers we have come up with to our series of questions and create from this raw material our character's history. During rehearsal, we constantly refer back to this history to help us figure out our characters actions and responses to the various situations in the play. Remember, there are no right or wrong ways to do this. Just be honest in your search and when in doubt, always go back to the text.

# Acting techniques and theatrical conventions

For those of you considering doing a performance of the play, here are some basic acting techniques and theatrical conventions to keep in mind.

### PACING SHAKESPEARE'S PLAYS

It is generally agreed that in Shakespeare's day his plays were performed with alacrity. The language moved and the action moved. With Shakespeare, perhaps more than with any other playwright, there is an acting technique that dictates that as soon as the last line of one scene is spoken, the first line of the next scene comes in hot on its tail.

Language is, after all, the critical element of Shakespeare, and we want all the action to come *on the language*—that is, with the words. This means that when a stage direction says "enter UL X DC," the language begins at the UL entrance (unless otherwise specified). Also, whenever possible, actors should be moving toward their exit with their last lines so that the action and language are continuous.

This does not mean that the actor has to feel rushed or be afraid to take pauses. It's just that for the most part, Shakespeare is best performed without indulgence. As Hamlet says to the players: "Speak the speech I pray you, as I pronounced it to you, trippingly on the tongue."

### STAGE ETIQUETTE

Another important element for our purposes in performing requires that after exiting from the stage, an actor proceed quietly and unobtrusively around upstage to his or her next entrance and then silently watch the action on stage until it is time to reenter.

Courtesy and cooperation are two of the most important elements in the theater. We work as a team and do all we can to assist our fellow actors and thereby help our production move along smoothly.

### MONOLOGUES

If your character has a *monologue,* you have some choices as to how to deliver it.

Depending on the situation, you could either talk directly to the audience and share your inner thoughts with them, or you could do the speech as though you were thinking out loud and the audience is overhearing you.

### ASIDES

An *aside* is often a bit of dialogue that the audience hears, but supposedly the other characters on stage do not hear. Benedick's asides during his gulling scene are examples of this type of aside.

When he is behind the arbor, he should just peek out from the side and deliver these lines to the audience. The others onstage merely go on as though they did not hear him. Note then that Claudio's line about Benedick having "ta'en the infection" is in response to what Claudio observes of Benedick, not what he has overheard.

Sometimes asides are directed to other actors, such as when Don Pedro, Claudio, and Leonato are talking to each other during the gulling scene and they don't want Benedick to hear them. These asides are best done by using a *stage whisper,* which the audience could hear, but Benedick could not.

### WHISPERING

A *stage whisper* differs from a real life whisper in that it must be loud enough for the audience to hear it clearly. Paying particular attention to your consonants will help immensely.

### A BEAT

A *beat* is a theatrical term for a second or two of silence used to accentuate a particular moment onstage.

### ANGLING OUT

This is a theatrical convention for making sure that the audience can see the actors onstage. In real life when two people talk to each other, they probably stand face-to-face. On stage it is necessary to stand on an angle facing slightly out to the audience in order to be seen.

When standing on the sides of the stage, it is often necessary for the actor who is nearest the outside to place him or herself a little below and on an angle to the actor who is closer to the center. This is done to make sure the audience can see the action. This is definitely something to experiment with.

## COUNTERING

*Countering* is adjusting your position on stage to accommodate or balance a movement made by another actor, such as when someone joins a scene already in progress or when an actor is required to cross from one side of you to the other. We do this to keep adequate spacing between the actors on stage so that the audience can get a clear view of the action.

## AD LIBS

When the term *ad lib* is noted in a script, it indicates to the actor that he or she must make up some words or dialogue to fill the moment.

Remember that whenever an ad lib is called for, it must be appropriate to the character and to the time in which that character lived!

## BOW

An Elizabethan bow is an altogether different animal from a modern one. The Elizabethan bows were very courtly and dashing.

Here's the general idea:

Elizabethan gentlemen rarely stood with their feet together, but rather struck a jaunty pose, with one foot slightly in front of the other and with one hand on their hip. They stood up tall, head high, eyes looking straight ahead and tried to appear very sure of themselves (sometimes too sure). Standing around with hunched shoulders, hands in the pockets, looking at the ground was a good way to get shoved aside!

The same proud attitude was maintained while bowing. The bow was a greeting—usually between equals—and not a slavish acknowledgment of superiority. (If a bow was made to a person of superior rank, the person of lower rank merely bent a little deeper from the waist.)

The mechanics of the bow are:

1. Step back a little with one foot, bending that leg slightly at the knee; keep the front leg straight.
2. As you hold your arms slightly open to the sides, bend forward from the waist—but not too much. Keep the back perfectly straight and the head in line with the back but perhaps at a slight angle.
3. Keep your eyes on the person you are bowing to (unless the person you are bowing to is royalty, then look at the floor!)

Circumstances and relationships will dictate how elaborate or simple a bow should be—so figure out what your character would do in the situation he finds himself in.

## CURTSY

A curtsy is very demure and simple. The lady would place one foot behind the other and shift her weight to sort of "sit" slightly on her rear leg, bowing her head, with her hands clasped demurely in front of her, or at her sides, palms forward.

When Beatrice demonstrates her curtsies in Act 2 scene 1, she may choose to exaggerate these moves.

## MUSIC AND DANCING

Unless you have a choreographer, several cast members skilled in Elizabethan dances, and musicians to play the *krummhorn,* keep the dances simple!

The party dance is really just an excuse for the characters to sashay around and flirt with each. The simplest dance to do this with is called the pavan. Before we learn the steps, let's practice attitude! Get into couples, men on the right. Men, hold out your left hands a little lower than shoulder high, palm upwards. Ladies, place your hands lightly on top of your partner's hand. Start with your feet together, then leading with your left foot, walk around the room. Keep your backs straight and heads held high—and flirt like crazy with your eyes and smiles.

After you've mastered this, stand with your feet together. Now step forward onto your left foot, then (keeping your weight on your left foot) bring your right foot up to meet it; next, step forward onto your right foot and (keeping your weight on your right foot) bring your left foot up next to it. It's sort of like walking with a slight pause at each step. Now practice walking around like this for a while.

The official way of referring to this is *step together, step together,* and so on. Once you feel comfortable doing this, stand with your feet together and do *step together, step together,* starting with your left foot. Then (starting with your left foot) take three regular walking steps forward and stop by bringing your right foot even with your left. Then start the *step togethers* with your right foot, taking the three steps and end with your feet together. Walk around the room like this for a while, alternating the starting foot. Congratulations, you've done it – that's the pavan!

This basic dance step (step together, step together, step, step, step together) can be done going forwards, backwards, in a circle, even *backwards* in a circle. When doing it in a circle, the partner on the inside of the circle takes small steps, or can even stand still while the partner on the outside moves around.

A variation (which is not legitimately the pavan) can be done stepping to the sides instead of forward so the actors can play a scene while they dance and not fall off the edge of the stage! We'll want to use this quite a bit in the *Much Ado* dance. For this: start with your feet together, then stepping onto your left foot, do two *step togethers* to your left foot, then take another step to your left with your left foot, now cross your right foot over your left foot and shift your weight onto your right foot, then take one more step to your left with your left foot, and bring your right foot to your left foot and stop. Now do all this to your right. (Clue: have someone read the preceding aloud and just follow the instructions — it's a lot simpler that way!)

The music for the pavan is slow and stately, in four-four time. You should go to your local library and ask the reference librarian to help you locate appropriate recordings of Renaissance music (it might be referred to as Elizabethan music, or 16th century music). If you've a musician in the group who plays the guitar, the recorder, the flute, or maybe a violin, there is an example of a 16th century pavan on page 170.

Here are some basic patterns that would work for the various couples:

Don Pedro and Hero—starting on Hero's line, "So you walk softly . . . ," Hero and Don Pedro do one complete pavan (step together, step together, step, step, step together) going forward and then one sideways to the right.

Borachio and Margaret—who will have stepped into the spot that Hero and Don Pedro vacated—do the same pattern on their lines, ending with Borachio twirling Margaret across him to the right.

Benedick and Beatrice—who have gotten into the ready position—do one complete pavan downstage, one to the right, one to the left, then Benedick stands still while Beatrice does four complete pavans circling him twice (this is what he will later refer to as standing at the "mark with a whole army shooting" at him!). They then end with one pavan to the left. This should time out so that the dance, the dialogue, and the music can all end on the word *melancholy*. (If there is more music, just fade it out.)

The dance at the end of the play is pure celebration. Find a piece of joyous, up-tempo music of the period (even a polka would do) and get in a large circle, holding hands. On Benedick's line, "Strike up pipers!," make one complete circle, skipping to the right, and then one complete circle to the left. Stop, get in a straight line across the stage, raise your hands on high, and take your bow!

## "What will serve is fit"

A SUGGESTED SET

For our purposes, a simple set that serves for all locales is best. We suggest a bare space with masking tape on the floor to delineate the space and no tape where the entrances and exits are supposed to be. When an actor crosses through these imaginary openings, he or she has *entered* or *exited* the stage.

The *set pieces* needed are two sturdy benches about forty inches long, one set down-right and one set in front of the *arbor*.

The arbor is established with two six-foot ladders positioned with their rungs toward the up-left corner of the stage and set about four feet apart. A piece of rope is tied from the outside leg of one ladder to the outside leg of the other across the top of the ladders. To this rope, attach a sheet (with large safety pins or clothespins, or stitch a pocket in the sheet through which the rope can be run).

In any case, you want to end up with a sheet concealing the ladders. This sheet should be painted with trees. The entire arbor could be decorated with vines or shrubbery, real or fake. What needs to be created is the idea of trees, that various characters can climb into (by climbing up the ladders) or hide behind.

With this as with all the other technical elements, simplicity is the key; with Shakespeare, language is the primary focus! See page 168 for a set diagram.

## "I'll show you some attires . . ."

SUGGESTIONS FOR COSTUMES AND PROPS

For our purposes, props and costumes should be kept very simple. This will not only make it easier to produce the play, but it will keep our focus firmly on the language, where it needs to be.

### COSTUMES

Think about how your character might dress if he or she were around today and find something appropriate from what you have easily available to you. You might check out the closets of others in your household and borrow from them, or your local goodwill store is another good source. Here are some suggestions, but don't feel constrained by them, this is only a starting place:

BENEDICK—a casual but elegant guy, he could wear slacks and a turtleneck with a blazer, which he wears, carries, or doesn't use, depending on the scene. After his gulling scene, he spiffs up, changing into a shirt and tie and adding a dapper-looking hat.

CLAUDIO—youthful, but a little more conservative than Benedick, he might wear slacks, a long-sleeved shirt, a blazer, which he, too, wears or not, depending on the scene.

DON PEDRO—he is royal and elegant and might wear a suit and tie with appropriate shirt. He might also wear a red sash going diagonally from one shoulder across his chest and fastened at his hip, as a sign of his royalty.

LEONATO AND ANTONIO—these older, distinguished gentlemen could wear suits of a more conservative nature, maybe even of an older style

DON JOHN—may want to express his sinister nature by dressing in very dark, somber colors, perhaps a dark suit, with a dark shirt, buttoned all the way up and no tie.

CONRADE AND BORACHIO—dark slacks and long-sleeved shirts to go with their master.

DOGBERRY AND VERGES—could wear very casual slacks and short-sleeved shirts with large trench coats over them.

THE SEXTON—he's been called from his work in the churchyard and could be wearing old slacks and an old shirt.

THE WATCH—pants and sweatshirts with some kind of jacket for warmth not style.

FRIAR FRANCIS—priestly looking, perhaps black slacks, black shirt, and a white collar!

THE MESSENGER—probably emulates Claudio, wears neatly pressed slacks and long-sleeved shirt, probably a tie, but no blazer.

BEATRICE, HERO, MARGARET AND URSULA—the women should all be dressed in skirts and blouses — long skirts if available. Beatrice's outfit should be of a vivid color; Hero's, pale; Margaret's perhaps slightly sexier; Ursula's more conservative. Hero adds a veil in the wedding scene, which could be as simple as a yard of sheer white fabric.

## PROPS

LETTER FOR LEONATO—this letter announcing Don Pedro's arrival need only be a sheet of white paper with writing.

MASKS FOR THE DANCE—these can be the simple toy-store type with elastic bands. Or each actor might design his or her own out of cardboard – painted and decorated with feathers, glitter, and jewels and attached to a stick held infront of his or her face. These can be outrageous and exciting—they are for a masked ball—great fun!

BOOK AND GLASS OF WINE FOR BENEDICK—the book can be a slim hard-bound volume; the wine glass of either plastic or sturdy glass; for the wine, grape juice or Kool-aid would work just fine.

PARASOLS FOR HERO AND URSULA—the smallest umbrellas you can find, hold them angled behind you rather than overhead so that the audience can see your faces.

BENEDICK'S SONNET, which he stuffs in his cheek—a clean piece of paper. Benedick will have to determine the size of the sheet that will work for him.

LANTERN—this could be a large flashlight or an actual lantern if available—it need never be lit.

MIRROR, VEIL, GLOVES, HAIRBRUSH—a hand mirror would be best for Hero to hold up as needed; the veil is the one described as part of Hero's costume; the gloves are the ones that Claudio gave Hero as a wedding gift and she will wear them at the wedding, so whatever you may have that is appropriate; the hairbrush—simple enough!

WEDDING BOUQUET FOR HERO—a few simple real or fake flowers would be lovely.

PAD AND PENCIL FOR SEXTON—any type will do.

SWORD FOR BENEDICK—if a real one is available—great! Otherwise, a toy-store type, or even a yardstick would do. When Benedick calls it a sword and puts his hand on it, we will believe it is a sword! Whatever it is, he can wear it in his belt.

COINS FOR LEONATO TO GIVE DOGBERRY—three or four ducats will do!

SONNETS FOR BENEDICK, HERO, AND CLAUDIO—Benedick's sonnet is probably on plain white paper. Claudio will have an identical one in the last scene. The one Hero stole from Beatrice's pocket might be on colored paper—even perfumed. Benedick might want to sniff it!

VEILS FOR THE LADIES IN LAST SCENE—these could be yard-long pieces of fabric that the ladies could place over their heads to conceal themselves. For safety's sake, you may want to use fabric you can see through.

# "A book of words"
GLOSSARY OF TERMS

THEATRICAL CONVENTION
An agreed-upon action (that may or may not be used in everyday life) that we *establish* on stage to convey something unusual that the script may require; asides are an example of theatrical conventions.

ESTABLISH
To set up a theatrical convention, such as when Benedick says his asides in the gulling scene and the actors onstage don't hear him. Once this is established the first time, the audience will accept this convention each time it occurs.

THEATRICAL LICENSE
Liberties we take with the script to achieve certain results that we as actors, directors, or editors are going for.

BLOCKING
The organized physical movement of a play.

REHEARSAL PROCESS
The time between the casting of a play and the opening.

READING
An organized, rehearsed presentation of a play in which the actors read from the script rather than memorizing the lines. (Could be done seated or with simple movements.)

SHAPE
A clear definable beginning, middle, and end to a scene or to the entire play. (Also referred to as arc.)

THROUGHLINE
This usually refers to the series of actions a character performs throughout the course of a play in quest of his desires.

CUT
To eliminate from the script.

VERNACULAR
Vernacular is defined by Webster's as "using a language or dialect native to a region or country rather than a literary, cultured, or foreign language." For our purposes, then, vernacular would be our everyday American English.

DOUBLING
When one actor plays two parts. For example, the actor playing the Messenger might alter his appearance and return as Friar Francis.

STAGE
The area designated as the space upon which the action of a play takes place.

ENTER
To walk into the area referred to as the stage.

EXIT
To leave the stage area.

CROSS (ABBREVIATED X)
To move across the stage to the area indicated by whatever stage direction follows the term. (Xing then means crossing in the stage directions.)

STAGE TERMINOLOGY
(Note that the following stage terminology is indicated from the point of view of the actor, onstage, looking out to the audience.)

**SR** The abbreviation for stage right. This means towards the right side of the stage as viewed by the actor when facing an audience.

**SL** The abbreviation for stage left—toward the left side of the stage from the actor's point of view.

**US** Up stage means toward the rear of the stage.

**DS** Down stage is toward the front of the stage.

**C** The center section of the stage.

We combine these terms to describe all the various sections of the stage. For example:

**DRC** down-right-center, which refers to the lower part of the stage to the right of center stage.

**DLC** down-left-center is the opposite of DRC

**UR** up-right is the upper part of the stage on the right side.

Use the chart on the next page to determine other designations. These designations are only approximate. If you are using the suggested stage directions, don't feel you have to stand dead center in the DRC circle if that is indicated—do whatever looks and feels best for your space and your production.

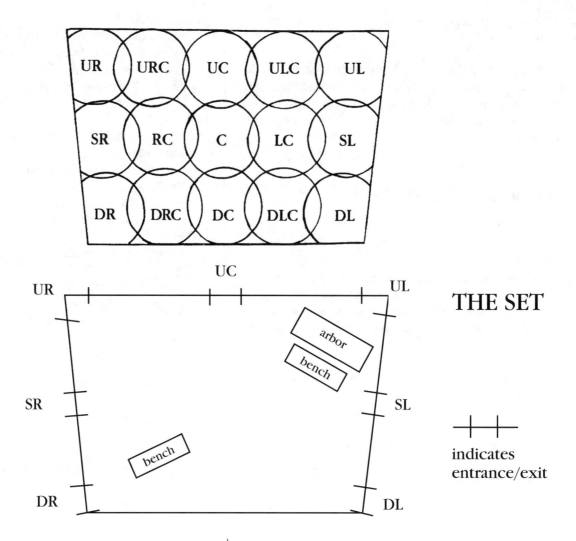

THE SET

indicates
entrance/exit

# Additional projects

1. Write a letter to your character's best friend and describe what's going on in your character's life at the moment. Tell your friend about the other people in *Much Ado*. What do you think of them?

2. Go to the library and find art books with pictures of the 16th century. Observe how the people of Shakespeare's time dressed, stood, and carried themselves. Observe their surroundings, their homes, and their facial expressions. (If you're lucky enough to live in a city with a museum, check it out.)

3. Write out the story of what happens to your character during the course of the play when he or she is not onstage. Where are they and what are they doing?

4. Look at a map of Italy and locate all the Italian towns that are mentioned in the play.

5. Observe people you come in contact with and notice their traits and idiosyncrasies. See if there are aspects of their personalities that you can "borrow" and incorporate into your character.

6. Write out a list of adjectives that best describes the various aspects of your character.

7. Make up your own Dogberry Dictionary. List words you have misused or heard misused in the past and their corresponding correct usages. (If you can't remember any—make some up!)

8. To test the reliability of *noting*, spread yourselves around the room so that you can't overhear each other. Whoever goes first will whisper a short story to the person nearby. That person will then go to the next person and whisper the story. Continue on and when the last person has been told, he or she will tell it aloud. See how reliable the transfer of information has been.

You get the gist. Come up with a project related to *Much Ado* that interests you and pursue it. The more we know about a play and its elements, the better we understand and enjoy it.

# Bibliography

*Eleanor of Aquitaine and the Four Kings*
Amy Kelly
Harvard University Press 1950

*The Sources of "Much Ado About Nothing":*
*A Critical Study*
Charles T. Prouty
Yale University Press 1950

*Broken Nuptials in Shakespeare's Plays*
Carol Thomas Neely
Yale University Press 1985

*Shakespeare and the Renaissance*
*Concept of Honor*
Curtis Brown Watson
Princeton University Press 1960

*Friends and Lovers: The Phenomenology of*
*Desire in Shakespearean Comedy*
W. Thomas MacCary
Columbia University Press 1985

*Shakespeare's World of Love:*
*The Middle Comedies*
Richard Courtney
Simon and Pierre 1994

*Shakespeare: The Comedies*
Ed: Kenneth Muir
Prentice-Hall, Inc. 1965

*Comic Transformations in Shakespeare*
Ruth Nevo
Methuen & Co. Ltd. 1980

*Agape and Eros*
Anders Nygren
Translated by: Philip S. Watson
The Westminster Press 1953

*Modern Critical Interpretations*
*William Shakespeare's "Much Ado About Nothing"*
Ed: Harold Bloom
Chelsea House Publishers 1988

*Love in the Western World*
Denis de Rougemont
Translated by: Montgomery Belgion
Pantheon 1940

*Shakespeare's Comedies:*
*From Roman Farce to Romantic Mystery*
Robert Ornstein
University of Delaware Press 1986

*Unconformities in Shakespeare's Later*
*Comedies*
Kristian Smidt
St. Marin's Press 1993

*The Art of Courtly Love*
Andreas Capellanus
Translated by: John Jay Parry
Frederick Ungar Publishing Co. 1959

*The Pelican Shakespeare*
*"Much Ado About Nothing"*
Ed: Josephine Waters Bennett
Penguin Books, Inc. 1958

*The Folger Library Shakespeare*
*"Much Ado About Nothing"*
Ed: Louis B. Wright and Virginia A. LaMar
Washington Square Press 1964

*The Oxford Shakespeare*
*"Much Ado About Nothing"*
Ed: Sheldon P. Zitner
Clarendon Press 1993

*The Variorum Edition*
*"Much Ado About Nothing"*
Ed: Horace Howard Furness
J.B. Lippincott Co. 1899

*Redeeming Shakespeare's Words*
Paul A. Jorgensen
University of California Press 1962

*Shakespeare and His Social Context*
Margaret Loftus Ranald
AMS Press, Inc. 1987

*The Arden Shakespeare*
*"Much Ado About Nothing"*
Ed: A.R. Humphreys
Methuen & Co. Ltd. 1981

*The Story of English*
McCrum, Cran, and MacNeil
Viking Press 1986

**170**

*Asimov's Guide to Shakespeare*
Isaac Asimov
Avenel Books 1978

*Shakespeare Lexicon and Quotation Dictionary*
Alexander Schmidt, revised Gregor Sarrazin
Dover Publications Inc. 1971

*The Meaning of Shakespeare*
Harold C. Goddard
University of Chicago Press 1951

*The Book of the Courtier*
*Baldesar Castiglione*
Translated by: Charles S. Singleton
Ed: Edgar de N. Mayhew
Anchor Books 1959

*The Plays of Shakespeare*
Ed: Howard Staunton
G. Routledge 1858–1861

*Popular Dances of the Renaissance*
Judith Kennedy 1985

# Pavan                    Luys Milan 1535